TABLE OF CONTENTS

"Ask veteran skiers about their most magical moments on skis, and nine out of ten will talk about powder: that certain morning, sparkling light, untracked slopes, feathery powder billowing up *over your head*! And afterwards, a perfect set of tracks is all that's left."

Backcountry Skiing
by Lito Tejada-Flores

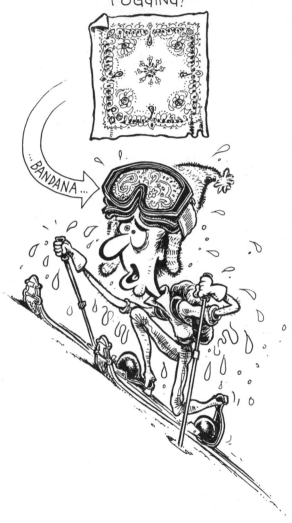

Allen & Mike's Really Cool
BACKCOUNTRY
SKI BOOK

Traveling and Camping Skills for a Winter Environment

IT'S COSMIC!

FALCON®

CHOCKSTONE

2 3 4 5 6 7 8 9 10 MG 03 02 01 00 99 98

ISBN 1-57540-076-6

PUBLISHED AND DISTRIBUTED BY

Falcon® Publishing, Inc.
P.O. Box 1718
Helena, MT 59624

DEVELOPED BY:

Chockstone Press

WARNING: BACKCOUNTRY SKIIING IS A SPORT WHERE YOU MAY BE SERIOUSLY INJURED OR DIE

READ THIS BEFORE YOU USE THIS BOOK.

This is an instruction book to backcountry skiing, a sport which is inherently dangerous. You should not depend solely on information gleaned from this book for your personal safety. Your backcountry safety depends on your own judgment based on competent instruction, experience, and a realistic assessment of your skiing ability.

There is no substitute for personal instruction in skiing and skiing instruction is widely available. You should engage an instructor or guide to learn backcountry safety techniques. If you misinterpret a concept expressed in this book, you may be killed or seriously injured as a result of the misunderstanding. Therefore, the information provided in this book should be used only to supplement competent personal instruction from a instructor or guide. Even after you are proficient in traveling in the backcountry safely, occasional use of a guide is a safe way to raise your proficiency.

There are no warranties, either expressed or implied, that this instruction book contains accurate and reliable information. There are no warranties as to fitness for a particular purpose or that this book is merchantable. Your use of this book indicates your assumption of the risk of death or serious injury as a result of skiing's risks and is an acknowledgement of your own sole responsibility for your backcountry skiing safety.

ACKNOWLEDGMENTS

The knowledge which made it possible for me to write this book is a synthesis of my own personal experience and all of the other people with whom I have had the pleasure of sharing the winter environment. Thanks must be given to my friends Kyer Wiltshire and Rowland Hill with whom I first ventured out in the snow. I would also like to acknowledge the National Outdoor Leadership School, for it was there as both a student and instructor that I really honed my skills. May all of those with whom I worked continue to share their experience: Jim Chisholm, Jim Ferguson, Mike Bailey, Reese Jameison, John Gookin, Willy Cunningham, Phil Powers, Greg Collins, Sue Miller, Patrick Clark, Maria Timmons, Jono McKinney, Dave Greenberg, Greg Wright, Eric Sawyer, Marit Sawyer, Kathy Lindholm, Gary Cukjati, Chris Lander, Aileen Brew, Andy Elsberg, Mike Wood, Bob Vallevona, Michele Tremblay, Lynne Wolfe, Marco Johnson, Rusty Wells, Chris Wahlberg, Rick Rochelle, Mark Roy, Missy White, Carl Siegal, Willy Peabody and others who I may have missed due to my failing memory banks. Thanks also to my many ski parners who are too numerous to mention.

In the writing of this book I would like to thank Abby Warner, Tom Hafnor, Molly Absolon and Don Sharaf who all took time to look over the text and help with the genesis of this whole project. In addition thanks to Tony Jewell and Matt Mitchell for reviewing the illustrations.

Finally a big hug and kiss to Lynn Morrison who gave me a helping hand whenever I asked, read text, reviewed first drafts and tried hard to understand my crazy ways. Thank you all.

Allen

I need to thank Evan Stone, my first backcountry ski partner. Evan also told me about this outdoor school in Wyoming called NOLS. I'm also forever indebted to Mort Drucker and Jack Davis, plus "the usual gang of idiots" at Mad Magazine for all of my art schooling. Also, many thanks to R. Crumb.

Thank you Allen for carrying that tiny note pad into the Wind River Range. This was the first ink to paper in the big job of creating this here book.

Mike

FOREWORD

Skiing is one of the most pure forms of play to be had in the mountains. Normally static humans slide down powdery slopes, bounce out pretty turns, or tumble in reckless, painless cart-wheels. Slippery skis, a bit of practice, and magical, ephemeral snow are the basic ingredients. Venturing further into the back country adds untouched powder and sparkling winter beauty to the fun. The extra effort of the trek in and the hill climbing loosens your muscles, heightens your anticipation, and makes the skiing seem even better.

As skiers venture further from lift-served front country, they need to understand and avoid hazards such as avalanches and extreme cold. Facing the prospect of unbroken snow on an open slope, the already puny human brain/ego can be diverted from even obvious danger by thoughts of carving turns through lightest powder. Even the clear clues to potential hazard – recent avalanche activity, heavy snowfall, or wind – get clouded by the excitement of perfect runs. Every year we read stories of skiers lost in avalanche during the beautiful sunny days that follow big snowfalls. Such days are crisp and energizing, but the deep snow is at its most taunting.

Walking the path between possible danger or discomfort and fun is an ever-present part of the game. The mix of serious informa-tion and fun in *Allen and Mike's Really Cool Backcountry Ski Book* mimic that path. No matter how much you think you already know about skiing, camping or traveling through the winter mountains, you will learn a new trick or two by reading this book that may mean the difference between a comfortable, fun day and one that is less enjoyable. Every idea may not appeal to you – I personally hate plastic bags on my feet – you'll have to pick and choose which ones you like and which you don't. But if you are like the group of skiers perusing these pages at my home the other night, you will find yourself saying, "I never thought of that" now and then as you read.

Mike and Allen may not have been at this game longer than any-one else, but they live and work in the cold, snowy Wyoming win-ter and want nothing more while they are out there than to be comfortable. They have sought and can offer the knowledge of more than a few skiers and winter campers in the mountains of Wyoming and Idaho. Read on and you can be a little drier and a little less tired on your next ski into the backcountry. You'll prob-ably have energy for a few more runs.

Phil Powers

INTRODUCTION

This book is for all those folks that have kept their alpine skis in the closet and instead have worked at the telemark turn, logging chairlift miles and impressing the locals with that "funny knee bend." Yet, they still feel there is something missing. That something is what telemark gear was originally designed for— the ability to get away from the lift lines and crowded slopes. The ability to ski in the backcountry and make tracks where nobody else has.

This book is also for cross-country skiers whose day tours seem to end too soon. Those who reach that point where they need to turn around and head back to the car, but keep on wondering "what is over the next hill." It is also for the already avid backcountry skier who has already explored the outer reaches of winter. We've skied and camped in the winter for years and have made enough mistakes now that we are sure to have learned something. That something is what we are trying to share with you. We hope you can learn from our experience just as we have learned (and keep on learning) from others.

Of course, there is no need to take all the advice in this book as the only gospel. For example, if your goals are to travel light and cover a lots of ground then you will want to modify some of the camping techniques to save time and lose some of the gear to save weight. Then again, if your goal is to establish a base camp a few miles into the mountains and ski all the surrounding country, you may consider using all the ideas here and then some. You can even pack your sled and backpack with decadent extras and make the trip a sheer extravaganza. Most likely your goals will be somewhere in between these two extremes, and with experience and time you will develop your own preferences of what gear you want to carry and the style that you like to camp in.

Remember, winter is a great time to be out. It happens to be our favorite time of the year. Maybe it's the cold, the whiteness of new fallen snow hanging on the trees or the solitude of a winter's night. There's just something about this time of year that is invigorating. And then there is the skiing. What a great sport!

Mike and Allen 1996

CAREFUL
how you Load
your SHOVEL
'cuz
if you fall
You can really
BONK yer HEAD!

SAFETY IN THE BACKCOUNTRY

The first time I ever went winter camping I knew almost nothing about what I was doing. I can remember standing there in the middle of this frozen lake after a sleepless night on the snow in my summer sleeping bag (I didn't have a winter bag or even an ensolite pad!) wondering if I would ever be warm again. My cotton turtle neck, wool sweater, and German Army issue wool jacket were no match for the cold clear skies, polar front and slight breeze that cut right to the bone. So while my friends decided to go climb a mountain—not my suggestion—I headed out the 3 miles to the warmth of the car.

There's no reason your first trip out has to be so brutal. A little knowledge and preparation can prevent all sorts of problems. Winter camping and travel should be fun. That's why we ski in the first place, because it's fun! The purpose of this book is to help you expand the possibilities of skiing beyond the lift lines.

Although winter is a great time of the year to be out, it is also an unfriendly time of the year to get hurt. Imagine dealing with a debilitating injury in deep snow when the wind chill is a howling -30 degrees. For this reason backcountry travelers need to be more cautious then lift area skiers. Maybe it's not a good time to jump off that 10 foot cliff and ski the tight line down through the trees. It is also a good idea to travel with a decent first aid kit and to have some knowledge of how to use all the stuff in it.

The focus of this chapter is on some common winter problems and safety. Because there are many good sources and books on first aid and avalanches, I will only summarize the information and hope that you seek out more knowledge as you build your experience base.

COLD INJURIES

There are three types of cold injuries the winter traveler should be aware of: they are hypothermia, frostbite, and immersion foot. These injuries tend to sneak up on a person and, before you know it, you're in a potentially dangerous situation. Because of this you need to have some knowledge of how cold injuries work and, more important, how to avoid or prevent them.

CONDUCTION

CONVECTION

RADIATION

EVAPORATION

RESPIRATION

As humans we **lose heat** through four mechanisms: conduction, convection, radiation, and evaporation. Out in the wilds, unless we build a fire or make hot water bottles, we **produce heat** in three ways.

Metabolism is the act of using the food we eat to produce the energy needed to throw snowballs or ski. The off shoot of this metabolism is heat production. That is why you will often feel yourself warming up after chowing down a good meal.

Exercise is another way we produce heat. "An active camper is a happy camper;" happiness is often a function of warmth. So if you're out there in the snow and you are feeling the strangle hold of cold, get up and go shovel some more snow on the shelter or go for a short but intense run through the snow. Exercise is the most effective way we have of producing heat.

Finally, we find ourselves *shivering* as we get cold. This is the body's way of telling us that we had better get busy doing something to warm up or else. It is also the body's way of producing heat. Unfortunately, not only is it uncomfortable and annoying, but it is inefficient and uses up our stored supplies of energy quickly.

HYPOTHERMIA

Hypothermia is a condition in which the core of our body is losing heat faster than we are producing it. This can happen in different ways and conditions, and it is not just limited to the winter environment. Our core temperature normally hovers around 98.6°F. When it drops below 95°F we enter the realm of hypothermia. In the medical world, hypothermia is classified as having distinct stages. To keep it simple, however, we can just say that as a person's core gets colder (as he or she sinks deeper into hypothermia) it becomes progressively harder to reverse the process and rewarm the person. Death will occur eventually. The problem is that the early stages of hypothermia, when it is easiest to reverse, are hard to recognize. Therefore, it is important to be on the lookout for the signs and symptoms both in yourself and in others.

People in the **earliest stages of Hypothermia** will feel cold and clumsy. They will exhibit improper behavior, such as not putting on a hat. Their personality will show changes, and they will become apathetic, listless or emotional. They may show signs of shivering, although there are many cases where people have passed through this stage without shivering. This is especially true when people have been exercising beyond their normal point of endurance. As hypothermia progresses, a person will start to lose his or her coordination and start to stumble. The person will be unable to do simple tasks, such as zip a zipper. He or she will show more marked personality changes and may become belligerent and irrational.

Shivering trying to make your body smaller

FIRST SIGNS OF HYPOTHERMIA

At this point, it is still possible to rewarm the person in the field. Just getting the person into warm and dry clothes and having him or her run around may do the trick. If not, get the person into a warm environment such as sleeping bags with one or two other warm people. Everyone in the bag should strip down to their lightest insulating layer so that heat exchange between their bodies will be maximized. Rescuers in the bag should switch out if they find that they are no longer warm. Hot water bottles close to the victim are also recommended but be careful not to burn the person. Food and water, preferably warm and sweet, should also be given to the hypothermic patient as soon as they can take it on their own. Don't forget about the others in the party; they should eat and drink as well to keep their strength up. Remember that a person who has been hypothermic takes awhile to recover and is more susceptible to relapsing within the first 48 hours after recovery.

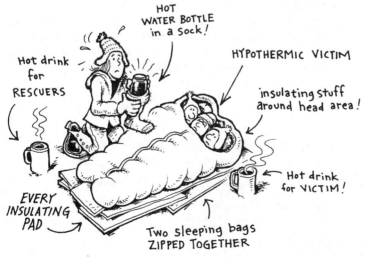

HOT WATER BOTTLE in a sock!

Hot drink for RESCUERS

HYPOTHERMIC VICTIM

insulating stuff around head area!

Hot drink for VICTIM!

EVERY INSULATING PAD

Two sleeping bags ZIPPED TOGETHER

If you miss these first signs of hypothermia then the person can go into severe hypothermia. In this stage the victim may not be able to stand up or communicate intelligibly. He or she may lose consciousness and eventually death will occur unless the victim is treated. At this stage it is almost impossible to warm the victim in the field, and it will be necessary to get medical attention. Care must be taken to keep the person from getting any colder. Treat the victim very gently as his or her heart can easily be thrown off its normal rhythm. There may be a chance for the person even if it appears hopeless. There have been amazing rescues in which hypothermia victims have appeared dead and have been successfully rewarmed after reaching a hospital. In the medical world the rule is that someone is never dead from hypothermia until they are warm and dead.

Prevention is the key to avoiding hypothermia. It is a matter of drinking and eating enough to keep the body well fueled and also being aware of your own and others' energy levels. Dressing properly is also important. The old adage that cotton kills has its roots in the fact that wet cotton has no insulating value and only cools the body more due to evaporation. Therefore, wear clothes made of polyester or wool. Remember to keep a watchful eye out for the symptoms of hypothermia so you can put a stop to it before it gets out of hand.

Frostbite is the freezing of tissue and can only occur when the temperature is below freezing. The chance of getting frostbite is increased with windy conditions and dehydration. Frostbite can be superficial or deep depending on how much tissue is frozen. It appears white or gray and feels cold and hard. The harder the frostbitten area feels the deeper the freezing. Rewarm under controlled conditions, by immersing the frozen part in water, between 101° and 108°F, until it is completely thawed. In many cases it is easier to evacuate the person keeping their injury frozen. This is especially true with frostbitten feet because pain prevents most people from being able to walk once the frozen area is thawed. Large blisters (known as blebs) will develop after rewarming and need to be protected from breaking open. The possibility of infection can also complicate the injury.

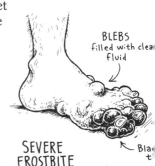

BLEBS
filled with clear fluid

SEVERE FROSTBITE

Bla
t

Frostnip occurs when the very outer layer of flesh is frozen. It happens most frequently in windy conditions to exposed areas such as nose, cheeks and ears. The skin appears white and can be rewarmed by placing a hand over the area and protecting it from the wind. Another form of frostnip is contact frostbite. Contact frostbite occurs when you pick up a cold metal object with bare hands. It is similar to sticking your tongue on a freezing dry object and can be avoided by always wearing thin liner gloves. Spilling super-cooled liquids like gas or alcohol on skin can also cause contact frostbite.

Prevention of frostbite can be easy, but it takes constant vigilance. A loss of feeling is one of the signs that frostbite has occurred. It is incredibly important to rewarm fingers, toes, ears, nose or other bodily parts when they begin to

feel cold and is essential before you lose any sense of feeling. Since circulation of warm blood is important in prevention, avoid tight-fitting clothes and boots and stay hydrated by drinking lots of fluids.

Hands and feet can always be warmed by placing them on any warm part of your body, or better yet, use your friend's belly! The idea here is to place the cold part right up on the warm skin of your friend's belly. Having skin-to-skin contact will provide the fastest amount of heat transfer. Other warm areas to stick cold feet and hands are the neck and armpits.

WET
SOCKS!

IMMERSION FOOT

Immersion foot (also known as trench foot) is a nonfreezing injury that occurs when your feet are cold and wet for extended periods of time. Permanent nerve and circulation damage can occur. This, in turn, can produce severe pain, especially as the foot warms up. It is difficult to detect immersion foot in its early stages, but as it progresses the foot feels "wooden" and may look shiny or mottled. As the foot is rewarmed it will tingle and become bright red and painful. Prevent this insidious injury by keeping feet warm, changing out of wet sweat soaked socks into dry socks once the day's activities are done, and **always** sleep with warm and dry feet. If your feet do not warm up after you have been moving awhile, stop and rewarm them on someone's belly

SNOW BLINDNESS AND SUNBURN

Additional injuries that winter travelers should be aware of are snow blindness and sunburn. Snow intensifies the sun's glare. Even on overcast days, it is possible to get a wicked sunburn. This is especially true of places where we usually don't get much sun, such as under the chin and the underside of the nose. Altitude will compound the problem because the intensity of the sun is greater due to less filtering of ultraviolet rays in the thin mountain air.

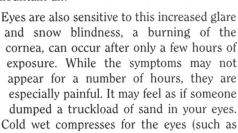

SOLAR RADIATION REFLECTING OFF the SNOW!

Eyes are also sensitive to this increased glare and snow blindness, a burning of the cornea, can occur after only a few hours of exposure. While the symptoms may not appear for a number of hours, they are especially painful. It may feel as if someone dumped a truckload of sand in your eyes. Cold wet compresses for the eyes (such as tea bags) and a dark environment can help ease the pain until the eyes heal. This recovery process may take a couple of days. It' s easy to prevent both snow blindness and sunburn by wearing sunglasses and sunscreen or a sunblock. Sunglasses with side shields offer more protection for the eyes at altitude.

AVALANCHES

Perhaps the most deadly force a winter backcountry traveler may encounter is that produced by the very surface you are skiing on...snow! Avalanches—both big and small—have buried, injured and killed innumerable people since humans began to travel on snow. Thus it is important to understand avalanche dynamics and know how to travel safely in avalanche terrain. You should seek out as much knowledge as you can on

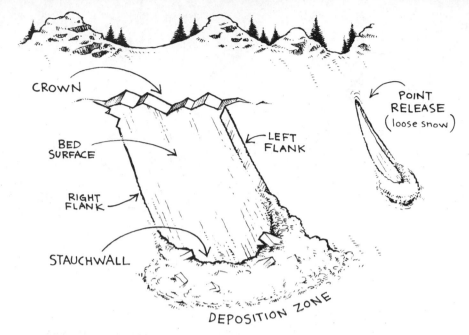

avalanches especially if what is being said here doesn't sound like just a quick review. There are many excellent resources on avalanches (see appendix), so we will touch briefly on only a few key things.

The two most common types of avalanches are loose snow slides and slab avalanches. **Loose snow,** or point release slides, most commonly occur on slope angles above 35 degrees. They normally start as a single point and pick up more snow as they slide down. Occasionally they get big enough to cause damage on their own, but for the most part they tend to be harmless. Probably the biggest danger from a loose snow slide comes from being swept away by one into unfriendly terrain, such as large cliffs.

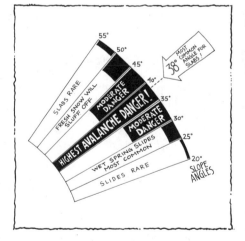

Slab avalanches most commonly occur on slopes between 30 and 45 degrees, although they have occurred on slopes with higher and lower angles. Between 35 and 40 degrees there is an even greater incidence of slab avalanches and more caution needs to be exercised. Slope angle is one of the most important factors in determining the potential for a slide. But it is difficult, even for experts, to guess the angle of a slope. So traveling with a slope-meter (clinometer), is useful in measuring this all important angle.

A slab is a layer of snow with internal cohesion greater then the strength of its bond to the layer beneath it. A problem

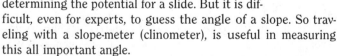

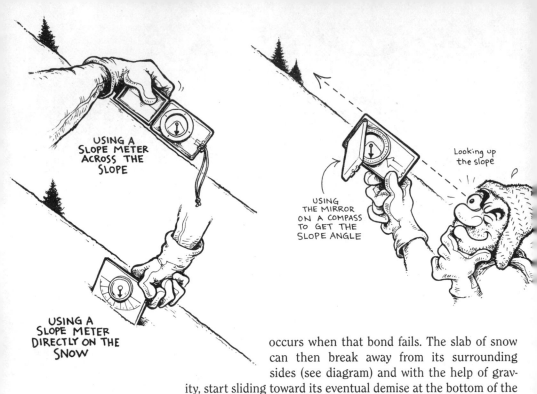

USING A
SLOPE METER
ACROSS THE
SLOPE

USING
THE MIRROR
ON A COMPASS
TO GET THE
SLOPE ANGLE

Looking up
the slope

USING A
SLOPE METER
DIRECTLY ON THE
SNOW

FRACTURE!

SLAB

SNOW PACK

WEAK
LAYER

GROUND LEVEL

SLIDING
SURFACE

occurs when that bond fails. The slab of snow can then break away from its surrounding sides (see diagram) and with the help of gravity, start sliding toward its eventual demise at the bottom of the slope. Let's hope you or no one of your acquaintance is traveling on it or in its path.

Slab avalanches can be hundreds of feet across and travel thousands of feet; or they can be just a few feet in width, and run only a short distance. Both kinds can bury and kill you. Slab avalanches tend to be insidious and hard to predict. The snow can be compacted and hard or light and fluffy. The critical factor is that it is poorly bonded to the surface below it. In the spring wet slabs, caused by melting snow or rain, become more of a problem. Wet slabs tend to slide on lower angles—slides at 20 degrees have been reported—and are very dense and heavy.

Slab avalanches are responsible for most avalanche-related accidents and are almost always triggered by the victim. For this reason alone it is important to understand how to lessen your risk of getting caught.

TERRAIN

If all you plan to do is ski in flat country—like Minnesota—you probably don't need to worry about avalanches. But as you head to the mountains, it's time to start looking at where you're going. As mentioned before, avalanches are most common between 30 and 45 degrees. Therefore if you avoid all steep terrain you don't have much to worry about. However in the age of plastic boots and fat skis you better learn to evaluate these steeper slopes because sooner or later that's where you'll want to be.

Slopes that are more likely to be avalanche prone are north facing and/or on the lee side of ridges. North-facing slopes are colder, so it takes longer for the different layers of snow to bond together. This means that weak (or sliding) layers in the snow pack will persist for longer periods of time. Lee slopes tend to be wind loaded, which increases the amount of stress

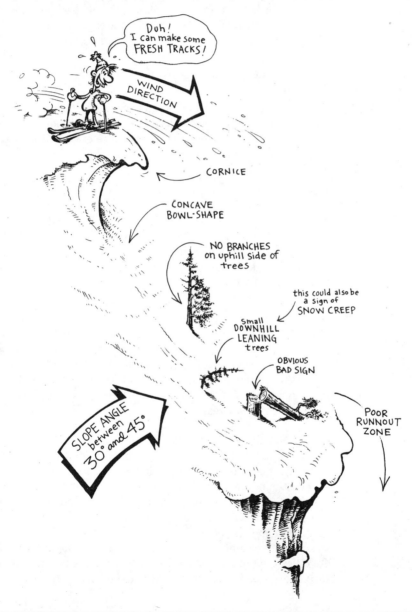

CONCAVE
SLOPE

CONVEX
SLOPE

on the snow pack (and stress is always a bad thing, just ask a postal employee). This is due to the fact that as the wind blows over a ridge it takes snow from the windward side and blows it to the other—or lee—side. Cornices also form on the lee side of ridges, and although they can be fun to jump off, they are prone to breaking off and setting off slides, so be wary of them.

The shape of a slope is also something to consider. Slopes with a convex shape tend to fracture easier then those that are more concave. This has to do with compressional forces that are higher in a concave shape. The more convex a slope the more likely it will be to fracture. While the break over line in an avalanche (crown) will usually be in an area of convexity, it is also possible to trigger an avalanche from the compressional zone.

Gullies often look like great routes to ski up, but if you are in the bottom of one when the slope above you goes, look out. Suddenly you have no where to go and neither does the snow. It piles up on you and then piles up on you some more. Gullies are some of the worst places to be because even a little snow can bury you deeply. It is much safer to follow the ridges, and besides you get a better view.

Treed slopes can be safer then open bowls as the trees can help anchor the snow to the slope. However, sparse trees can also be the "connect the dot" points for the fracture line of an avalanche. Slides can also start on slopes above a stand of trees and run right through them, the strainer effect. So don't put all your faith in trees. I like to think of trees as something to hold onto in case I happen to be standing by one when the snow starts moving.

Trees can also offer you clues as to possible avalanche paths. Lots of small flexible trees in the middle of a slope could be telling you that the snow slides pretty often there. Similarly look for trees that show signs of broken branches on their uphill sides. Huge pine trees ripped out by the roots and lying in a tangled mass at the bottom of a slope is also a bad sign. I would avoid these areas.

STAYING OUT OF TROUBLE

Wouldn't we all like to stay out of trouble? To do so we need to always be aware when traveling in avalanche country. A friend of mine was once buried after a long day of skiing. He and his friends were skiing back to the car and not paying attention to what was above. All of a sudden a slope above them slid, and they found themselves caught. Luckily one of them remained unburied and was able to unbury my friend. Together they rescued the other two in the party. They were fortunate to walk away from that one, but had they been pay-

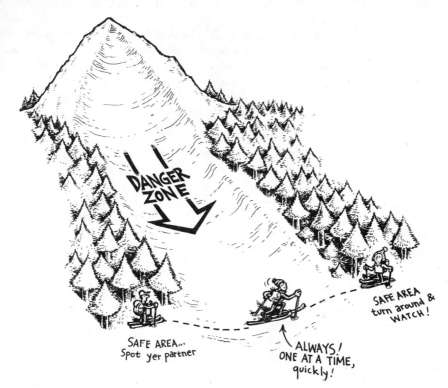

DANGER ZONE

SAFE AREA...
Spot yer partner

ALWAYS!
ONE AT A TIME,
quickly!

SAFE AREA
turn around &
WATCH!

ing more attention to where they were going they could have avoided the accident altogether.

When skiing in the mountains, it's important to always look for the safest route. There is an art to choosing safe routes, and it takes time and practice to develop this skill. One suggestion is to pencil in your potential route on a topographical map before skiing into unfamiliar terrain. This helps you to microanalyze the map and the route you are planning to take. It is amazing how much detail you can pick out doing this and how often you will be able to identify likely trouble spots. Similarly, it is also amazing how many small slopes or terrain traps you can miss. But as you do this more and more, you'll miss less and less. Of course for this to work you must be familiar with how to read a topographic map. So get a friend to teach you or take a course on this invaluable skill.

Try to avoid traveling in gullies, especially steep-sided ones. Watch out that your path doesn't bring you to the bottom of a big avalanche slope where you won't be able to assess the stability of the slope safely before crossing it or ascending it. Staying on the tops of ridges, where they aren't corniced, is the safest route. As stated earlier, routes that stay in the trees are often safer then ones up an open slope. But if the route through the trees is below a possible avalanche slope, it may not offer much protection. For this reason it is a good idea to know where your route leads. Map skills really are invaluable!

WUMP!

(an obvious warning
sign...)

When crossing or skiing potentially dangerous slopes, **it is important to go one at a time from island of safety to island of safety.** That way if the slope does fail, only one person would be caught and the others can spot the last place that person was seen. This will help with finding and rescuing them if they are buried. Of course, this only works if you are looking out for each other.

SLOPE EVALUATION

When traveling on the snow be constantly aware of what is happening with the snow around you. Some warning signs to watch for: fresh avalanche debris on surrounding slopes, cracks in the snow shooting out from under your skis or the snow under your feet collapsing or "whumphing." If you are noticing any of these signs, then maybe it's not a good day to ski those avalanche-prone slopes. In fact, sometimes it may be the perfect day to be at home reading a book. Frequently, on the day following a big storm, very unstable snow conditions can exist, and you should take a lot more care and time assessing dangerous slopes.

Weather is also a factor to keep an eye on. Is the wind blowing strongly? Is it snowing heavily? Conditions may be changing, and what was safe earlier may no longer be as stable. On those first few days following a storm you must be careful not to let the desire to get the first tracks or those face shots take priority over your safety. Assure yourself that the slope you want to track is indeed stable. I would hate to have my ski season cut short by death.

Therefore, it's good sense to come up with a protocol for evaluating the slopes you want to ski in the backcountry. Any time you ski a slope above 30 degrees you are taking a risk and you should evaluate that risk. Digging pits and performing rutschblock tests will give you an idea of the different layers in the snow and how stable they are. It is important to also find out how thick the potential slab is and how wide spread the potential sliding layer is. A 6-inch slab on the surface is unlikely to be really dangerous, while a widespread sliding layer is more dangerous than isolated pockets. Avoid slopes where a rutschblock yielded a stability factor of 4 or less. At a 5, stay away from slopes above 35 degrees and think hard about those above 30. These tests

THE RUTSCHBLOCK

Pick a slope representative of the one you want to ski. It is best is to dig on the slope you want to ski, but you need a safe spot as you don't want the slope to go with you on it! Your test site needs to be on the same aspect and angle as what you want to ski and needs to be similar in elevation. Dig a pit similar to the illustration and go through the following steps to evaluate it.

score	Degree of stability	Force applied
1	extremely unstable	fails while digging the pit
2	extremely unstable	fails while approaching or stepping onto the block
3	very unstable	fails while down weighting the skis
4	unstable	fails with one jump
5	potentially unstable/ marginally stable	fails with two jumps
6	Relatively stable	fails after repeated hard jumps
7	Stable or very stable	doesn't fail

are not hard and fast rules. Slopes that have scored a 7 have failed, but it should help you assess the relative stability of a slope and then you can factor in the other information such as the different layers in the snow pack.

Rutschblock tests, slope angle and shape, "whumphing" sounds, shooting cracks and the weather are all factors that point to the big picture and must be used together to assess the potential for avalanches.

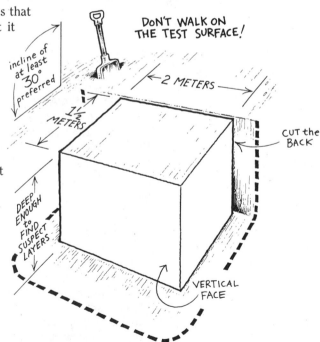

DON'T WALK ON THE TEST SURFACE!

incline of at least 30° preferred

2 METERS

1½ METERS

CUT the BACK

DEEP ENOUGH to FIND SUSPECT LAYERS

VERTICAL FACE

IF YOU ARE CAUGHT!

Someday you or one of your ski buddies may get caught in an avalanche. Then you will damn well want to know what to do! First of all if you were following the guidelines about crossing potentially dangerous slopes one at a time, then only one of you should be caught. If you find the snow around you suddenly moving then you should yell to alert others. This will ensure they will come looking for you.

Next you should try and jettison your gear, such as skis and poles, because that stuff drags you down and you want to stay on the surface of the snow where you will have a better chance of surviving. If you have a large pack on, bail on it too, but keep a day pack on as it offers protection for your back should you hit something. Also a light pack may help you float up in the snow, and more importantly, you may need the stuff in the pack if you survive the avalanche.

FIGHT TO STAY ON TOP!

SWIM IN IT!

Third, fight like hell. By "swimming" or flailing your arms and legs you create more buoyancy which helps keep you high in the sliding snow. The only exception to this might be if you were in heavy timber where the trauma of hitting a tree would out weigh the benefit of floating. In this case roll up into a ball and protect your head. When you feel the snow start to slow down throw one arm across your face to create an airspace (hopefully you kept your mouth shut so it didn't pack with snow) and reach for wherever you think the surface might be with your other hand. Having a hand above the snow could help your buddies find you faster.

If you are lucky, you will find yourself on the snow surface when everything stops. But if you find yourself under the snow your best chance comes from relaxing and hoping your friends will find you. Avalanched snow usually sets up so hard there is very little chance you will be able to move. Since sound doesn't travel well in the snow, in most cases you'll be better off saving your energy rather then yelling for help. There have been a couple of cases though where searchers located buried victims who yelled. If your searchers are close by, it might be worth shouting.

REACH UP
WITH ALL YOUR MIGHT.
give your rescuers
something to find!

If you happen to witness someone about to get caught in an avalanche, yell to alert him or her and anyone else around. Then watch them and try to identify the last place you saw the victim. This will be an important point in determining where to start looking for him or her. Next, make sure it is safe for you to go look for the person. Nothing could be worse for you (or them) if the potential rescuers get buried by another avalanche. If it is safe, then start your search. Depending on the number of people available and the size of the slide, any number of options are possible. Some things that need to get done are a visual search of the slide and debris. In this search,

COVER YOUR
MOUTH TO KEEP
FROM CHOKING ON SNOW!
Create an air pocket
if you can.

get rid of your skis
IF YOU CAN.

SAFETY IN THE BACKCOUNTRY

rescuers look for possible clues in the avalanche debris as to the whereabouts of the victim. These should get marked. Also make sure they aren't still connected to the person: A glove may have a hand in it.

A transceiver search should be started right away. This is the fastest method of locating someone who is completely buried, and since an avalanche victim's chance of survival decreases rapidly over time, it is important to find the person as soon as possible. That's why you should own and to know how to use a transceiver. Read the instructions that come with them, take a class and practice, practice, practice! Make sure the other searchers turn theirs off, or it won't do you any good. Probe poles can help pinpoint the victim's location. All searchers should stay and search for the person since going for

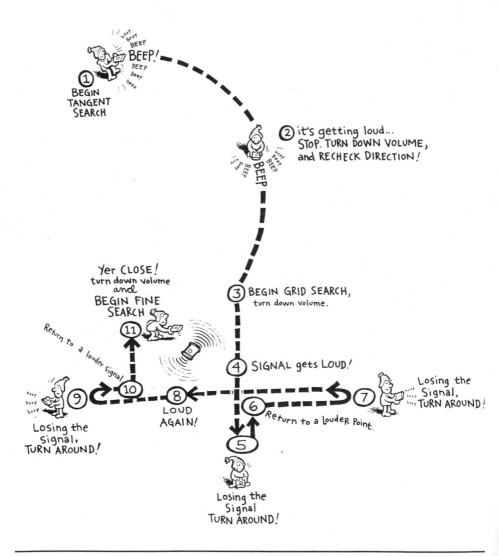

help prematurely will reduce the amount of personpower available for finding the victim. Only after a significant amount of time has passed with no luck in locating the person is it worth going for help.

PROBING

Probing can be done with specially made probe poles (see page 28), or if none of these are available, skis and regular ski poles will work, although they are not as effective or efficient. By removing the basket on a ski pole you will have a practical, though short, probe. If for some reason a person can't be located via a transceiver search then probing for them becomes the next best option. Try probing in likely spots first such as around trees where they might be hung up or in the toe of the debris in line with their last spot seen and any clues you found. Probing is usually a last-ditch effort, but it has worked.

Once you find the victim, those first aid skills you learned will come in handy. Make sure the person has an airway and can breath; then remember that hypothermia is probably close by. We wish you the best of luck and hope this never happens to you, but be prepared.

Take some first aid courses, know all that you can about avalanche conditions and carry the right equipment. Preparation is the first line of defense. Paul Petzoldt, pioneering mountaineer and the founder of the National Outdoor Leadership School (NOLS) used to talk about the six Ps: Proper Preparation Prevents Piss Poor Performance. By being prepared we lessen the chance of something going wrong, and when it does go wrong we have a better chance of dealing successfully with the problem.

One important thing I have discovered is to always do a transceiver check at the beginning of a ski tour. Make sure all those beepers are beeping. More than once someone's transceiver wasn't working before we ventured into avalanche terrain.

EMERGENCY GEAR

A first aid kit is always a handy thing to have along. There are many different formulas for what should go in them, and it is best left up to personal choice. At a minimum, carry a roll of athletic tape and some 4 x 4 gauze pads, but it might be better to bulk this out a bit, especially for extended trips. Just be wary of the first aid kit that gets so big nobody wants to carry it, so it gets left behind all the time. Better to carry a skimpy one than none at all.

BIVY GEAR

In the same vein I always carry a few things with me in case I should have to spend the night out. It's a small package and is not noticeable in my pack.

- Vegetable tin (for melting snow for water)
- Lighters and/or matches
- Down parka
- Leather man (knife and pliers)
- Candle
- Small "shortie" ensolite pad
- Fire starter, such as steel wool soaked with wax
- Space blanket

I figure with this bare minimum of stuff I could always light a fire and make some hot water. By standing between the fire and the space blanket you get reflected heat as well as direct heat. I have a friend who once used this method to warm up a hypothermic person.

IMPROVISED LITTER

Ski injuries most commonly occur to the legs. For these and other injuries that would prevent someone from skiing out of the backcountry, it is worth knowing how to build a litter. You should be able to make a litter with the standard stuff you carry. Use the patients skis and poles, some parachute cord or lash straps and a shovel. Lash it together as illustrated and pad with ensolites, parkas and packs. You will need something to tow with. If the skis don't have holes in the tip then you will have to drill them with a knife or awl. An improvised litter will work in a pinch, but they are harder to drag then a real sled and should not be used for someone with a possible spinal cord injury.

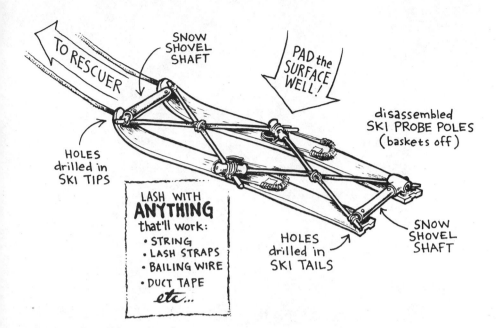

TO RESCUER

SNOW
SHOVEL
SHAFT

PAD the
SURFACE
WELL!

disassembled
SKI PROBE POLES
(baskets off)

HOLES
drilled in
SKI TIPS

LASH WITH
ANYTHING
that'll work:
• STRING
• LASH STRAPS
• BAILING WIRE
• DUCT TAPE
etc...

HOLES
drilled in
SKI TAILS

SNOW
SHOVEL
SHAFT

ITINERARY

It's always a good idea to tell someone where you are planning to go and when you should be back. You want to ensure that someone will come to the right spot looking for you should you be late. This is especially true for an extended trip in the wilderness. I will often write out a schedule and give it to someone I actually trust to remember and contact the appropriate people to come looking for me if I don't show up. With all these plans it is a good idea to have an expected time of return and a "freak time." The freak time is when you would actually want people to start looking for you if they hadn't heard from you. This could be hours or days from the time when you actually hoped to return depending on the length of the trip and its remoteness.

A NOVICE WINTER TRAVELER
(being miserable)

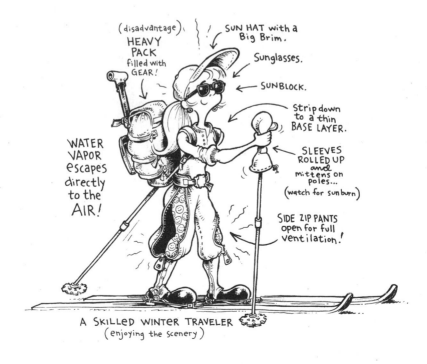

A SKILLED WINTER TRAVELER
(enjoying the scenery)

EQUIPMENT

Equipment. Now here is a touchy subject that everyone and their grandmother has an opinion about. The problem is that none of these opinions match and what works for one person may not work for another. This includes Mike and me, and since we rarely agree about any specific piece of equipment, its pretty hard to make recommendations that someone else won't object to. One person's essential is just another techno doodad to somebody else. Another issue that clouds written discussions on gear is the fact that technology is changing so fast that soon after I write this, something will change and people will assume that I am a dinosaur talking about such outdated equipment. So to avoid these pitfalls, Mike and I have decided to make general observations about gear and give you some options from which to choose. For the most recent discussion on specific types of gear we recommend you check out the many ski magazines that do reviews and are much more up to date.

SKIS

If you want to go backcountry skiing a pair of these are pretty much mandatory. Of course not everyone goes winter camping on skis, some slog it out on snowshoes and others prefer a snowboard over those long skinny things. There's just no accounting for taste. For myself, skis are the ultimate traveling device when snow is on the ground. They keep you on top, let you climb up hills and best of all, let you glide back down them. I personally prefer a fat ski over really skinny skis as they give more flotation for skiing powder. Others might like skinnier skis for faster travel on the flats. It depends on what you enjoy and your style of skiing.

OLD-TIMER   YOUNGSTER

In general a back country ski needs a softer flex than an area ski. This will allow the tip to rise up in the soft snow instead of bury itself below the snow surface. The lighter the ski the easier to haul around out there but you might lose something in durability. There are literally tons of skis to choose from and almost any of them will work fine, though they may have little variations. For the pocketbook conscious I would look for some old alpine boards with a soft flex. If they still have some life in them, great! If not they will feel a little dead, but they should work fine until your financial status improves. A

NEVER
PICK the ICE
out of your
BEARD!

EEEK!

Simply allow it
to gently
melt away,
this is much less
irksome.

few years back, I gave a friend a pair of boards that had I declared dead and she is still out there shredding it up on those skis and waiting for the day when I will give her another pair. In the end it just depends on how fussy you are.

Sidecut is the difference between the width of the ski at its fattest points (the tip and tail) and its narrowest point at the waist (middle of the ski). The more side cut a ski has, the faster it will turn. On the other side of the coin, skis with less side cut are better for touring since they will hold a straighter line.

SKINS

Skins are long thin pieces of nylon, mohair or rubber that attach to the bottom of your skis with glue and/or straps. Originally they were made from seal skin thus the name. They allow you to slide your skis forward but due to a number to backwards pointing hairs don't allow your skis to slip backwards. Like petting a dog, your hand slides easily down from head to tail but encounters resistance going the other way. There are two general types of skins on the market now, glue-ons and strap-ons.

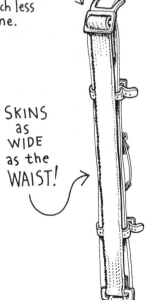

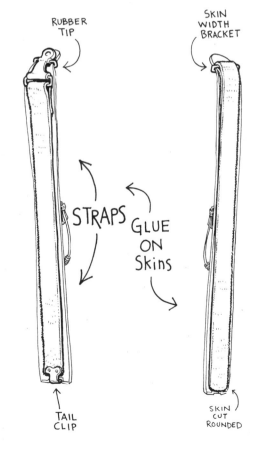

SKINS
as
WIDE
as the
WAIST!

adjustable
TIP

RUBBER
TIP

SKIN
WIDTH
BRACKET

STRAPS GLUE
ON
Skins

SNAKE
SKIN

TAIL
CLIP

SKIN
CUT
ROUNDED

Glue on skins are nice in that they stick to the skis and give maximum purchase for climbing a really steep skin track. They also tend to glide better than strap ons. A disadvantage is that they need more care and need to be reglued periodically. Also if the glue gets snowy (or really cold), it doesn't stick to the skis as well. Many people bring along some duct tape so that they can tape the skins in place in case of glue failure. For long trips in the backcountry you need dry them out from time to time.

SCRAPING OFF
the CAKED—on SNOW
from the sticky
side of yer SKINS

Strap on skins such as snake skins are easy to use and don't require much maintenance. They are also cheaper than glue ons. On the down side they tend not to glide as well and may not climb as well, especially on old hard packed trails or in spring conditions. Since I like to wax whenever possible, and use skins only for climbing the longer hills, I have a certain affinity for the low maintenance of strap ons. They are also nice for long trips since they won't require much care.

Important! Skins need to be the right size for your skis to get maximum climbing performance from them. If they are considerably narrower than your skis, they will not give you as much traction as they would if they were the same width as the skis. To find the right size measure the ski at its narrowest point (the waist) in millimeters. This is the width of the skins you want.

BINDINGS

As of this writing there are basically three types of bindings for backcountry skis. Three pin bindings and cable bindings for the true free heel skier and randonnee set ups for those who still prefer to lock down the heels. The advantage to the last is the increased control and stability for extreme type skiing. They will also accommodate plastic mountaineering boots, which is all I have ever used with them. Having used randonnee gear just for mountaineering approaches though, I am certainly not the best source of knowledge about them. Heck, I didn't even lock down the heels.

LOOK!
Three
little pins!

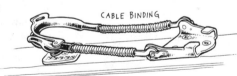

CABLE BINDING

Three pins bindings are amazingly simple and very light, perhaps their biggest advantage. They work well and hold the toes of the boots very snugly and were my binding of choice until I started breaking the pins off every month or so. In general three pins are pretty durable, but they definitely can't take the abuse a cable binding can so if you are a heavy and aggressive skier who lacks finesse (like me) then you might be better off with cables. You

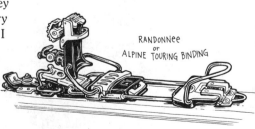

RANDONNEE
or
ALPINE TOURING BINDING

also need to be diligent about cleaning the snow out of the pin holes in your boots in order to get the pins in. Otherwise you can strip out the holes in your boots.

Cable bindings have definitely gained in popularity during the last few years. They are durable and offer more rigidity in a binding than straight pins. However they may not hold the toe

SKI LEASHES:
these are mandatory
at any lift area...
(*DAMN LAWYERS!*)

BUT these are a
potential death trap in
avalanche terrain!

TAKE 'EM OFF!

of the boot as securely as a pin set up. They also tend to release easier than pins. This bothers some people but I personally like this fact since it means I am more likely to leave them behind in case I get caught in an avalanche. The worst binding set up for releasing in this type of scenario are combo pin cable setups. These bindings offer the advantages of both pins and cables, but because they don't tend to release I would probably avoid them for the backcountry.

> **Cable and pin bindings are NOT RELEASABLE BINDINGS. They can (and often do) release in a bad fall or if you're caught in an avalanche. They are designed to clamp on and stay clamped on, so don't rely on them like you would a releasable alpine binding.**

BOOTS AND GAITERS

Boots may be the most important part of any skiing set up. You would be better off buying a good pair of boots before dropping a lot of cash on other pieces of gear. For one, they are the link between your feet and the skis, thus they influence what you can do with the ski. Second, our feet are very important to our ability to move around so we should keep them happy. Therefore, it is worth having warm and comfortable boots for whatever you chose to do.

SHORTY LEATHER
comfy & light

HEAVY-DUTY LEATHER

Boots come in all shapes and materials now, from beefy plastic boots with lots of buckles to lightweight leather boots that feel like slippers. The type of boot you choose depends on what kind of skiing you like to do and your own personal aesthetics. The new line of plastic boots definitely offers lots of downhill performance and durability but doesn't have the feel of a leather boot. I have long been a fan of a certain pair of lace-up leather boots. I enjoy the lightweight compared to most buckle boots and like the feel for the skis and snow conditions I get with them. This year, however, I finally broke down and bought a pair of petroleum products. They have been warm, comfortable and give me lots of

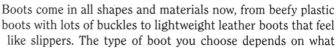

LEATHER
with STIFF UPPERS
and BUCKLES

LEATHER DOUBLE BOOT
WARM!

PLASTIC
Double boot

control in all types of snow conditions. I definitely enjoy skiing them, but at times I miss my leather boots for their feel and the honesty they demand of my technique.

For general all-around touring a pair of leathers is the way to go. Double boots will definitely be warmer then singles and have the additional advantage that you can get away with sleeping with just the inners versus the whole boot. If you are a downhill freakazoid like myself then you may want to consider plastics for the control they can add to your skiing. Hard-core vegetarians may also want to avoid having dead animals on their feet. (Ahh, but is petroleum so much better? Cows are a renewable resource at least.)

**PLASTIC Double
MOUNTAINEERING**
these fit alpine touring
bindings...

Gaiters are designed to keep snow and dirt out of your boots. In the winter we needn't bother with the latter and have a preponderance of the former. Knee-high gaiters will work best for keeping out snow if you are postholing around camp. Make sure they can be secured in such a fashion that the snow will not push them up off the boot. For overnight trips I would recommend tube gaiters or gaiters with beefy zippers. My experience has been that Velcro and/or tiny zippers ice up after awhile and don't work so well. Some ski pants have a gaiter incorporated into them but you should check that this will actually function when booting it.

GAITER

Supergaiters work great in the winter and add warmth to the boot as well. If the toe keeps popping off then you can glue it down. I find that epoxy, barge cement and shoe goo work great for this. At the end of the season, just pull the rand back up and store with the toe free to help keep the boots from curling.

SUPER-GAITER

SKI POLES AND PROBES

Something must be lacking in my knowledge of ski poles. I go with the cheapest pair I can find and they seem to work just fine. I guess there is something to be said about a pair of well balanced poles, I'm just not sure what it is. I do own a pair of adjustable poles but I usually don't adjust them, since just moving my hand placement on the pole works fine and is less time-consuming. But not everyone shares my little quirks. The advantage to adjustable poles is the ability to make them longer for touring and then shorten them for ski descents.

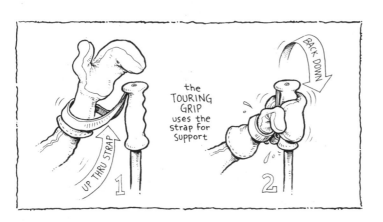

the TOURING GRIP uses the strap for support

UP THRU STRAP

BACK DOWN

1

2

HOLD IT HIGHEST by gripping the top

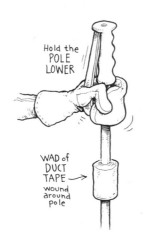

Hold the POLE LOWER

WAD of DUCT TAPE → wound around pole

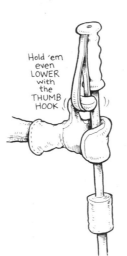

Hold 'em even LOWER with the THUMB HOOK

HOLD it LOWEST by gripping the DUCT TAPE

LAZY MAN'S way of changing your POLE "LENGTH"

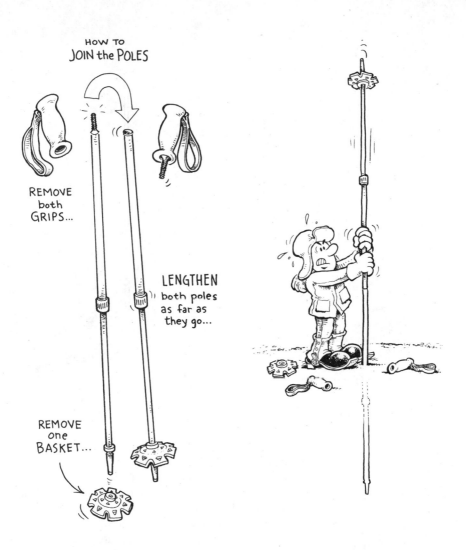

HOW TO JOIN the POLES

REMOVE both GRIPS...

LENGTHEN both poles as far as they go...

REMOVE one BASKET...

Poles that convert into probe poles are also nice, especially if you know how to put them together. There are a number of people I have met who have no idea how to change their poles into probes! In a pinch you can always pull off the basket of any pole and probe with it. I prefer a true probe pole over convertible ski poles. They tend to go together faster and probe down through the different snow layers easier.

ADJUSTABLE POLES

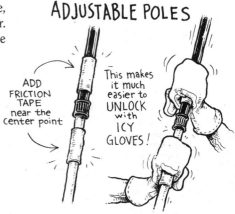

ADD FRICTION TAPE near the center point

This makes it much easier to UNLOCK with ICY GLOVES!

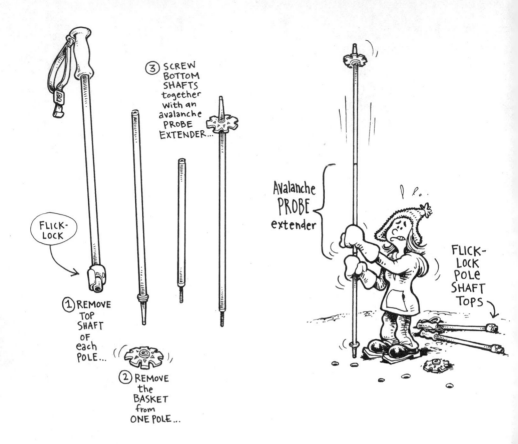

③ SCREW BOTTOM SHAFTS together with an avalanche PROBE EXTENDER...

FLICK-LOCK

① REMOVE TOP SHAFT OF each POLE...

② REMOVE the BASKET from ONE POLE...

Avalanche PROBE extender

FLICK-LOCK POLE SHAFT TOPS

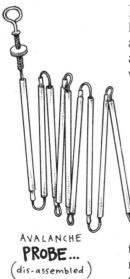

AVALANCHE
PROBE...
(dis-assembled)

PROBING TIPS

Probing with a converted ski pole or an actual probe is a valuable rescue skill (see page 19). It's important to make the effort and take some time to practice. You can do this by working with a partner, have them bury something large (like a backpack) with an avalanche beacon inside. Remember to make sure the beacon is turned to transmit, or you may not find it until spring. When burying, make sure it's at least four feet deep. First, practice probing only, so you can feel the subtle difference between hitting bottom and hitting the pack. Then practice searching in combination with a beacon and a probe. Together these two skills can dramatically increase your rescue time. But you need to practice!

Caution: Be careful if you're probing on a real victim search! You'll be amped up on adrenaline, and you'll want to move quick. But you don't want to hurt your ski buddy who might be only a few inches below the snow. Remember what mom alway said about playing with a pointy stick.

LURKS

Lurks are long staffs that skiers used before two poles became all the rage in the late 1800s. A single lurk, between 4 and 7 feet in length, is all the skier uses, planting it in the snow with both hands in the same rhythm you would normally use with two pole plants, crossing over the skis to plant it down hill each time. The first time I found myself lurking was when I broke one of my poles two days back in the wilds of the Wind River Range. By extending my one good pole I was able to ski out comfortably and developed an appreciation for this old style of single pole plants.

The LURK!

STORE-BOUGHT HEEL LIFT

HEEL LIFTS

These nifty little devices can make going up steep skin tracks a pleasure. Well maybe not a pleasure, but they do make it easier by raising your heel off the ski, which takes some of the strain off the calves. There are a number of different options to choose from. Some people swear by these little things while others prefer to stretch out their calves. I use mine about 50 percent of the time just because I have them. One important thing to remember is to pop them off before taking off down the hill unless you enjoy extreme skiing on 30-degree slopes.

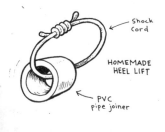

Shock cord

HOMEMADE HEEL LIFT

PVC pipe joiner

Some HEEL LIFTS attach directly to your skis!

The PVC HEEL LIFT fits nice just under your boot heel notch!

KNEE PADS

To protect our fragile knees from rocks, partially buried trees or the tops of our skis, knee pads come in handy. Wearing them under your wind pants will keep your knees drier as they have a tendency to collect snow. All you need to learn your lesson is one good smack on your kneecap; from this harsh moment on you'll never ski again without some serious knee protection.

Wear knee pads UNDER your wind pants...

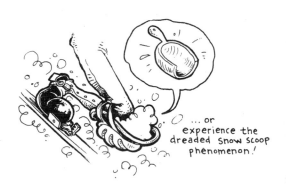

... or experience the dreaded snow scoop phenomenon!

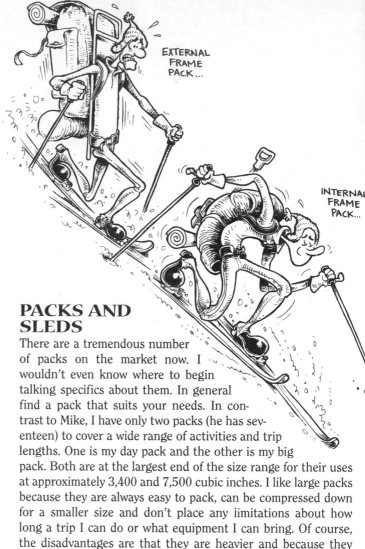

EXTERNAL FRAME PACK...

INTERNAL FRAME PACK...

PACKS AND SLEDS

There are a tremendous number of packs on the market now. I wouldn't even know where to begin talking specifics about them. In general find a pack that suits your needs. In contrast to Mike, I have only two packs (he has seventeen) to cover a wide range of activities and trip lengths. One is my day pack and the other is my big pack. Both are at the largest end of the size range for their uses at approximately 3,400 and 7,500 cubic inches. I like large packs because they are always easy to pack, can be compressed down for a smaller size and don't place any liimitations about how long a trip I can do or what equipment I can bring. Of course, the disadvantages are that they are heavier and because they allow you to pack whatever, they can get really heavy.

My daypack compresses down easily for those day tours I do, and by expanding it to its fullest potential and putting the top lid on, I can use it for two- to three-day trips. For trips longer than that I go to the big guy. Its top lid converts to a fanny pack for tours away from camp or the pack can be compressed down to a more reasonable size.

In general, internal frame packs work better for skiing than external packs because they keep the weight closer to your body so it is less likely to swing around and throw you off balance. The simpler the design of a pack the less that can go wrong with it. Ease of packing is also important in the winter as nothing is worse then having to fit everything carefully into its own compartment during a snow storm.

DAY TOURING PACK
(with shovel pocket)

BIG MULTIDAY PACK
(with strapped-on shovel)

EQUIPMENT

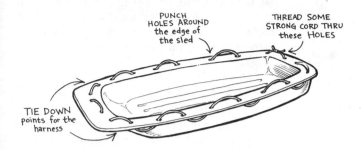

PUNCH
HOLES AROUND
the edge of
the sled

THREAD SOME
STRONG CORD THRU
these HOLES

TIE DOWN
points for the
harness

Sleds or pulks, as they are sometimes referred to, are nice in that they allow you to get the weight off your back. They can be of a fancy design with an attached cover or they can be as simple as one of those kiddie sleds that you get at hardware stores and attach a rope to for towing. Large-zippered duffels work great for keeping the gear in and can be lashed easily to the sled.

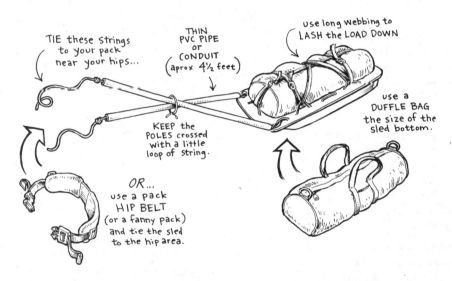

TIE these strings
to your pack
near your hips...

THIN
PVC PIPE
or
CONDUIT
(aprox 4½ feet)

Use long webbing to
LASH the LOAD DOWN

KEEP the
POLES crossed
with a little
loop of string.

Use a
DUFFLE BAG
the size of the
sled bottom.

OR...
use a pack
HIP BELT
(or a fanny pack)
and tie the sled
to the hip area.

Rigid bars between the harness and sled are nice for skiing down hills as they keep the sled from hitting your Achilles tendon. It is also nice to have bars that let you steer the sled with your waist. Crossing the bars between the sled and your hip harness adds an amazing amount of steering control; this is a big advantage when you thread your way through tight trees.

Sleds are great for long expeditions because you can really load a lot of weight into them. I have used them extensively on nine-day- to month-long trips and have never regretted having one along. One exception to this, might be if you are traveling in steep terrain, where having this beast swinging

It's LOTS
EASIER to TURN
with your hips
WITH CROSSED POLES
on yer sled!

around can compromise your safety or your sanity. Also if I decide to take a sled on trip where I could be carrying it on my back some of the time then I would definitely go with a kiddie sled as it weighs the least.

REPAIR KITS

As per Murphy's Law nothing will go wrong until you have absolutely no chance to fix it. For this reason alone it is always good to carry some type of repair kit. At its most basic my repair kit consists of some duct tape, bailing wire and a leatherman-type tool. For day trips this is plenty and allows me to fix anything enough to get back to the road. For longer trips however it would be a good idea to beef this up some since having to duct tape your boot to your ski each day would be a drag. Listed are some potential repair kits and some ideas as to what they might contain. Each person's needs may vary, but you should have enough to at least jury-rig a solution to most problems.

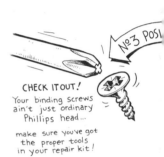

CHECK IT OUT!
Your binding screws ain't just ordinary Phillips head...

make sure you've got the proper tools in your repair kit!

SNOW SAWS

These are useful for building snow shelters and in snow pits for isolating columns of snow to find potential sliding layers. I have used a number of different ones and they all have worked well. My current favorite is one from Wasatch Touring that attaches to the end of my ski pole. This is a nice added touch for cutting the side of rutschblocks.

SNOW SAW

SHOVELS

These are absolutely mandatory when traveling in avalanche country. There are a number of breakdown backcountry ski shovels on the market. Find one that works for what you want to do. The smallest ones work well for day trips but won't move much snow for winter camping. They also have the disadvantage of not moving much snow when digging for an avalanche burial. Larger shovels will move a lot of snow but are heavier and bulkier. I favor a

LIGHTWEIG
AVALANCH
SHOVEL

So you can ALWAYS carry your shovel!

midsized shovel with a telescoping handle. It seems to be a good compromise and the extendible handle makes throwing snow easier on the back. In addition to attaching the shovel to my pack, I like to be able to sling it over my shoulder should I need to carry it without the pack. Some webbing tied between the blade and the handle does the trick for me.

TENTS AND TARPS

Now here is a can of worms. The debate over which tent is the best and whether or not tarps are superior to tents will rage on until eternity. Who really cares. Tarps, also called flys, are at the simplest just big rectangular pieces of coated nylon. Their biggest advantage is that they are much lighter and cheaper than tents. They can be strung up between two trees and staked out to the snow. Then with a little imagination and snow excavation a nice little enclosed shelter can be built. An even fancier tarp is Black Diamond's Megamid that can be pitched with a pole in the center, eliminating the need for trees. In the snow you will need some type of platform or base for the pole to keep it from sinking into the snow.

Tents have the advantage of being free standing. They also tend to hold up better in severe storms. For the winter I recommend a four-season tent. Tents with vestibules are nice for storing gear but will weigh more and may have more poles to dink around with. In cold weather I have had poles freeze together making them hard to break down. Even worse is when the elastic shock cord in them freezes while they are folded up. When this happens it looses its elasticity and you will have to piece the poles together, a very time-consuming process. In any event if your shelter of choice is a tent then make sure to have spare zipper pulls along or else you might just end up with a fancy tarp.

For winter camping single-walled tents can be nice and are much lighter. Since you are dealing with snow you don't need to worry about them leaking, although the walls will frost up more than a double-walled tent. They tend to be very expensive, as well.

STOVES

Butane, white gas, plate burner versus port burner—what does it all mean? Well, let me try to sort it all out. Butane or cartridge stoves burn fuel that vaporizes naturally in our atmosphere. Because of this you can just turn the valve on and light

BUTANE STOVE

them. White gas or liquid fuel stoves need to be primed or heated up to vaporize the gas before they will burn properly. Although at a disadvantage because of the increased time and trouble to prime them, liquid fuel stoves burn hotter, are less costly to buy fuel for and don't require as much packaging since you don't need to buy a new cartridge each time. In addition, butane stoves, even with an isobutane fuel mix, don't work as well in cold temps whereas white gas stoves will work just fine. White gas is probably the way to go for most winter campers. If you decide to go with a liquid fuel stove for winter camping then avoid those without pumps. In the winter pumping the stove to build the pressure within the fuel tank is a necessity.

WHITE GAS STOVE

Homemade customized stove pad

WATCH OUT

If you use white gas and plan to carry it in the 1-gallon cans, be sure to keep them upright. This helps to reduce the chance of them leaking. On a Denali Expedition I remember passing a group and looking in their sled. The gas had leaked out of the can, which was placed on its side, and was sloshing around inside the sled. Luckily they didn't have a lot of food stored in that sled. Gassing your food is very unpleasant. Not only will it taste awful, you run the risk of getting violently ill (just ask Mike!). Always do whatever you can to keep gas containers upright and as far away from food as possible.

Stoves with a plate burner such as the MSR's XGK burn loud and hot. The roar produced by them is comforting to some but tends to make conversation difficult. Stoves with ported burners (Optimus 111 hiker, for example) are much quieter, and although they may not boil a pot of water as fast, what's a few seconds compared to a stove that sounds like a jet taking off?

Another feature to look for in stoves is reparability. There's nothing like having to take a stove apart when it's 20 below. For this reason I like a stove with as few parts as possible. I will take a risk here and say that my favorite stove of all time is the MSR Whisperlite. It is a simple stove that is light, compact and tends to work well. It does have its idiosyncrasies but don't we all. Also for those critics who say these stoves don't simmer well, I answer that the key to getting any stove to simmer well is to avoid overpressurizing it when using the pump.

Stove pads are invaluable in the winter to keep your stove from melting into the snow pack. They can

Don't try to cook directly on the snow 'cuz the stove is gunna sink!

be as simple as a board big enough to put the stove on, to fancier contraptions.

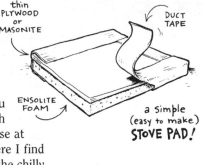

thin PLYWOOD or MASONITE

ENSOLITE FOAM

DUCT TAPE

a simple (easy to make) STOVE PAD!

SLEEPING BAGS

In general what you are looking for here is a four season bag that has a rating of 10 degrees or colder. If you are a cold sleeper then you are looking for a much warmer bag. I have a friend who becomes semicomatose at night and he uses a –40-degree bag to stay warm where I find that I can get by with a –10-degree bag myself here in the chilly Rockies. The rating system really has nothing to do with how cold it can be out for you to be warm. It is just a standard way of comparing different bags to one another. Loft is what you are really looking for. The more loft a bag has the more dead air space it creates for insulation and the warmer it will be. Different types of fill will loft more or keep their loft longer so keep these things in mind when looking at bags.

As for fill, or the ingredients within a bag, there are many choices out there. The biggest difference is between down and all the other synthetic fills. Down is great for compressibility, weight, loft and durability. It is quite spendy, however, and just think of all those cold duckies out there with no feathers. Another downer about down is that when it gets wet it stays wet and all that loft disappears like leaves in the fall. Mike likes to think of it as a nylon bag filled with pancake batter. (But if you keep them dry, they are so much nicer to stuff on a cold morning!!) Synthetic bags don't suffer from this malady and are the way to go if you live in wet climates or dread the thought of ever getting your bag wet. The different synthetics vary in the amount of compressibility, weight, loft and durability they have and in the price.

GoreTex–covered sleeping bags had been touted by many companies that make down bags but unless you seal all the seams (a tedious task at best) they really won't shed water and even then they probably won't survive a good drenching. Dry loft is the current covering of choice.

Sleeping pads will make a huge difference in sleeping warm since you lose most of your heat through conduction to the ground. There are many choices of sleeping pads out there from the deluxe inflatable thermarest to the simple foam pad. The only thing you don't want are simple open cell foam pads as they will compress under your weight and leave you on the ground. Closed cell pads like ensolite or evazote avoid this problem by retaining their shape thus trapping dead air within them.

Bivy bags or bivouac sacks are usually GoreTex and coated nylon bags that go over your sleeping bag to protect it from

---

rain or snow. They tend to work pretty well especially when new. They also add about 10 more degrees of warmth to a bag by adding extra protection from the wind and some more trapped air space. If you are planning to always sleep in some type of shelter, they aren't all that necessary, but they are nice for sleeping under the stars.

Finally, if you think you are a warm sleeper try out a lighter bag; but if you hate sleeping cold then get a warmer bag with more loft. There are few things worse then spending a long winters night out shivering in your bag.

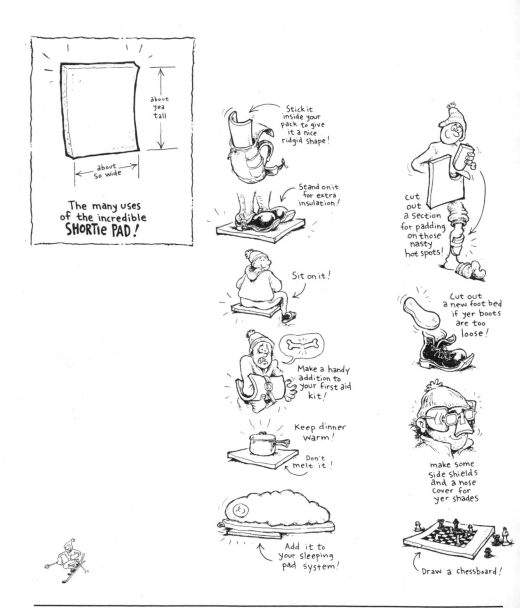

SKIING IN THE BACKCOUNTRY

Why bother skiing in the backcountry? Is it really worth the effort when you could be riding the lifts for max vertical? I certainly think it is. There's a certain satisfaction to making your own way to the top of a slope and then cutting the first tracks. Knowing that they will still be there when you get back to the top. There is also the quiet and solitude of the backcountry that you won't find at a ski area. What I also enjoy about the backcountry is breaking my own trail, sweating and toiling up the hills. This is the ultimate aerobic workout and the reward of a great downhill run couldn't be better. Plus it's just plain cool to be out there finding your own way, looking at the animal tracks and not worrying about getting creamed by a snowboarder—hopefully.

Skiing in the backcountry will present plenty of new challenges to the area skier. Not the least of which is the snow itself. Unlike the snow at an area that has a solid base created by diesel-fume-spewing Snowcats and thousands of other skiers, the snow in the backcountry can be variable. This means it comes in many different consistencies (light powder and wind slab to mashed potatoes) and will change from aspect to aspect, day to day. For this reason it can be easier for the novice skier to learn how to make tele turns at an area before heading out to the great untracked regions of the world. There are many books out there on how to tele turn and all the ski magazines run at least one article a season on freehill skiing. But the only real way to learn how to turn is to actually go ski! A friend or paid professional can help speed up the process by giving lessons in the fine arts of getting those boards to turn. A warning, however: Friends are often not the best at teaching these fine arts with an unattached view toward your learning, and we would hate to see any broken relationships.

OFF PISTE
In the backcountry there is no guarantee you will find perfect snow. Learning to ski (and fall) in all sorts of different conditions,

**THE ALL-IMPORTANT
STARTING POSITION**

such as a breakable crust, bulletproof wind slab or mush is part of the challenge of skiing away from the lifts. There are also those perfect snow days, with magic "hero snow" where you can do no wrong. But suddenly things change and we are humbled yet again. This is what keeps us on our toes and also what makes skiing in the backcountry so enjoyable. So the next step for those with at least a semblance of a turn is to get out there on the unpacked or, to use the French term "off piste," snow. I will limit myself to skiing in powder-type conditions. Techniques for skiing in the crude and crusty snow conditions are better left to books like Paul Parker's *Free Hill Skiing*, which emphasize all the different ski techniques. Spring conditions or corn snow will feel similar to groomed slopes.

Have you ever heard the phrase "bottomless powder"? Sometimes that's how it feels when you're out there getting ready to do your first turn. The most common mistake I see in people who are skiing off piste the first time is putting too much weight on the front ski. This usually leads to the ski diving into the snow pack and the skier doing a beautiful face plant if not a full on forward roll (which can be graded in much the same way as a diving competition).

When skiing on hard pack it's normal to weight your front ski more; this gives a positive edge, but as the snow becomes less consolidated your skis need to be evenly weighted, so they act as a platform. This platform helps keep you up in the snow pack and gives you something to jump off of into the next turn. I often get people to concentrate on weighting their back ski when skiing in deep

SHORTEN
POLES
for a nice
stable position
Low in your
tele-turn...

powder. This helps give them the feel for even weighting the skis and gives them more control over their back ski.

In the end, all it takes to be able to ski well in the different conditions possible in the back-country is time skiing the different conditions in the backcountry. My friends tell me that you have to fall a thousand times before you stop falling; I have discovered that

...or
LEAVe
LON
and
you'll
UNST
high
the

this is indeed true and through extensive research it seems that it's a thousand times on each type of snow encountered before I can say I have mastered it. But that's just the name of the game in the backcountry so don't be afraid to give it a try.

SHORT FALL

Well-padded area

UPHILL FALL

THE FINE ART OF FALLING

Falling is indeed a fine art and, as I always tell beginners, the surest way to stop. It is much safer to have a controlled fall then it is to ski wildly and take a digger in which you have no control of where or how you land. The best way to fall is in a sitting position off to one side. This you land where we humans have the most padding. It is also the easiest fall to get up from. So when you find yourself rocketing down a slope without any control, or you miss that crucial turn in the trees, just sit back and relax. When you stand back up you can pull it back together again instead of having your friends pull you out.

To get back up after a fall in deep powder, take your poles off and then lay them in an X flat in the snow. Pushing down on the middle of the X keeps your arms from diving into the snow. If your skis happen to be uphill, roll over so they are downhill and across the fall line before trying to get up.

EXTRA LONG FALLING DISTANCE!

Floppy Heels!

Poorly padded area

DOWNHILL FALL

SKIING WITH A PACK AND SLED

Oh yeah, eventually the goal is to get out in the backcountry for a few days at a time, which means carrying a pack. Some people may also want to pull a sled, depending on the length and type of trip. There are a few tricks here. One is to go light. The lighter the load the more comfortable it is to carry and the easier it is to ski.

Skiing with a pack isn't all that different from skiing without, except that the weight will change your center of balance and cause the skis to sink deeper into the snow. With time and practice you will get used to this and fall less often, but it takes awhile. The challenge of falling with a pack on is getting back up, especially from a face plant. It might be best to take your pack off and then get back on your feet.

A sled is a different story. The advantages of sleds are that they take the weight off your back. This makes skiing long distances over relatively flat ground and low angle slopes more enjoyable. On steeper slopes, however, the sleds often develop a life of their own, and this alien life form is not entirely human-friendly. Some people I know will swear that sleds know judo.

GETTING UP in deep powder snow

make a platform with CROSSED POLES

STOMP!
The
UPHILL SIDE
OF THE SKIN TRACK!

Create a nice
level trench,
so the sled doesn't
tip over.

When skiing uphill with a sled you will find that it wants to pull you back down the hill. Therefore, you can't climb as steeply as you can unencumbered. If I am looking at a day of hill climbing, I will either use very sticky wax or skins. Sleds make switchbacking or sidehilling more difficult. Often the sled will jump out of the track created by your skis. This leads to the inconvenience of the sled hanging down hill and off to your side as you try to break trail across the fall line. This discomfort is further enhanced by the trees that the sled will then try to embrace, leaving you wondering why you even bothered to bring the beast along. The solution to this problem is to create a wider track for the sled to travel in. Break the trail a second time with the uphill ski outside of the previous track to create a good sled trail.

Some sled and harness designs let you steer the sled with your hips. With these types of sleds, turn your hips out toward the fall line to get the sled to steer in toward the hill, lessening the chance that it will jump out of the track. Also when maneuvering around trees or rocks, rotate your hips toward the obsta-

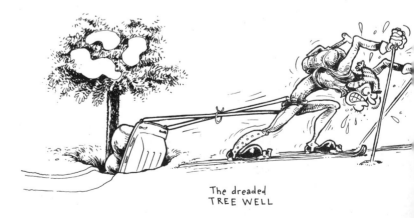

The dreaded
TREE WELL

TIE the TIPS together... use a strap, string, or even a Bandana

BE READY to snag every tree branch you walk near...

COMPRESSION STRAPS HOLD YOUR SKIS Keep the toe binding plate ABOVE a strap

BE PREPARED TO BONK the back of your legs...

Some packs have **WAND POCKETS** for things like tent poles...

use these for skis and you'll get a REALLY TALL top heavy load, impossible in trees and wind!

TIPS for carrying them SKIS ON YOUR BACK

cle as you turn around it to make your sled follow in your ski track.

Doing a kickturn on a hill with a sled is perhaps one of the least pleasant experiences you can have. Because of the sled's position behind you it is impossible to do a downhill kickturn. Therefore the uphill kickturn becomes the only option. With sleds that have rigid poles this kickturn is an exercise in yogic contorsionism as well. About halfway through this turn is when the sled usually decides to jump the track and start back down the hill, taking you with it. If you manage to survive the turn without plummeting down the hill, the next challenge will be to get the sled back in the track behind you. Like a big semi-truck trailer, the sled follows a tighter radius turn than you and will come out of the turn downhill of the track. I try to climb above the track a little to persuade it back into place. This is no easy exercise.

The best advice I have ever heard about skiing downhill with a sled is to always ski faster then the sled. This way you can avoid the troubling scenario of having the sled pass you. Since the sled is usually connected somewhere behind you this invariably leads to the sled taking you down. Some people recommend slow wide turns as you travel down the slope to keep the sled under control. Others advise a more direct route with lots of quick short turns to stay in control. In the end, it depends on your style of skiing, how good you are and the snow conditions. There may be times when conditions call for a long downward traverse followed by a kickturn followed by another traverse. Sometimes it might be better to walk down. Other times, as in wide open unobstructed bowls with a good runout, it might be appropriate to let the sled take its own line while you ski down unencumbered.

If all this makes you wonder why in the world you would ever want to go skiing with a sled, then just think about how a pack that weighs 100 pounds feels. Sleds are great for longer trips or for keeping your pack light on shorter trips. Once you learn a few tricks for handling them I think you will find it hard to go camping in the winter without one.

Route finding with a sled is an art that takes time and experience to develop. The most important things to keep in mind are to look for the mellowest terrain, avoid areas with thick vegetation and avoid sidehilling and kick turns like the plague—or at least whenever possible. Look for those places where you can turn around by making wide step turns.

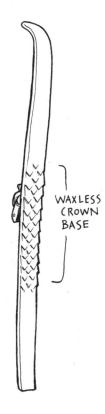

WAXLESS CROWN BASE

WAXES AND SKINS

Wax and skins are two devices we can use on our skis to give us the kick or stick we need to travel uphill or over flat ground. There are also skis that come with a patterned design on the bottom (crowns or fishscales) that allow the ski to glide forward but offer resistance to it moving backwards. These waxless skis can be used with skins for steeper climbing and are popular in some places. They would be very useful in areas where the snow is warm or temperatures change dramatically. But they tend to be slow and hum on the downhills and aren't necessary in colder climates.

My experience with waxes are all pretty utilitarian. The way I look at it there are two basic ways of waxing: the hard-core racing way—with zillions of different waxes and special techniques for applying them—and the dirtbag way. I am in the latter camp.

WAXING FOR DIRTBAGS

There are basically two types of waxes: glide wax and kick wax. Glide wax is what you put on your skis to go fast. Any book on ski tuning will talk about waxing the skis with this stuff. I pretty much hot wax and tune my skis at the end of each season and then scrape off the excess wax in the parking lot moments before leaving to do a run at the start of the next season. If I am having a conscientious year, I will also tune and wax my skis a few times during the season.

Kick wax is what I really want to talk about. This is the stuff that we can put on our skis to kick and glide with. A kick wax, in its most basic form, is a mix of paraffin and resin. The more paraffin the harder the wax and the colder the snow it should be used for. The more resin a wax has the softer and stickier it will be. Softer wax is meant to be used on warmer older snow.

This works because cold snow can be considered as very sharp (the snow crystals are well defined and pointy), therefore, it will stick into a hard wax when the ski is depressed into the snow. However, the wax is hard enough that the crystals only stick somewhat into the wax, then when the ski is unweighted the crystals become unstuck and the ski can glide forward. If you use a soft wax for cold snow, the snow crystals penetrate too far and the crystals don't break off and you get snow sticking to the skis, which doesn't allow you to glide. With warmer snow the crystals are not as sharp and won't penetrate a hard wax. Thus, if you get no stick and no kick, you need to use a softer wax.

There are probably about 30 different types of kick waxes. They are color coded for their use on different temperatures of snow (see illustration). The warmer colors such as red and yellow are used on warmer snow. For really cold snow use green. Blue is a little warmer or softer than green. To make things even more complicated and to get you to spend more money, there are also special and extra colors. For example, my two favorite waxes happen to be Special Purple and Extra Blue. A special

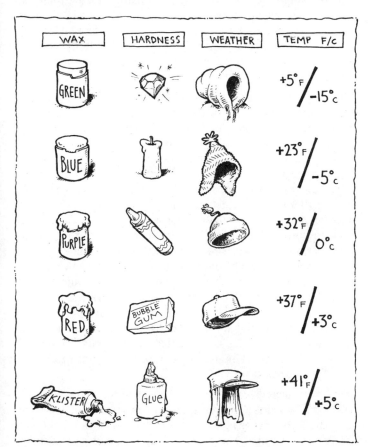

"SPECIAL"
GLIDE
colder

"EXTRA"
KICK
warmer

putting on
KICK WAX

WAX POCKET!

color indicates that it is for slightly colder snow. So special purple would be slightly colder and harder then purple. An extra by the same token is slightly softer and warmer than its corresponding color. Think of it this way, a special wax gives you that special glide while an extra gives you that extra kick or extra stick.

Klisters are a special, very sticky, form of wax for use with really old or warm snow that the harder waxes don't stick to well. To be honest, I must admit ignorance to the use of klister having only used it once. It was not an enjoyable experience for me, and I soon found that my hands and skis were sticking to everything. Since then a friend of mine has mentioned that cleaning is easier if you put duct tape on the bottom of the skis and apply the klister over it. All you have to do is peel the tape off.

Now the peanut-butter-and-jelly theory of waxing says that you should never put a hard wax over a soft wax. Just like you would never put the jelly on a piece of bread and then try to smear peanut butter over it. You should avoid putting on a soft wax thinking that you can easily put a harder wax on top of it. So if you are planning on experimenting with different waxes to see what will stick then err to the harder wax first. If that doesn't provide enough stick then put on the softer wax. That way you won't wind up with snow stuck on the bottom of your skis and a glob of wax to scrape off.

Now really hard-core wax geeks will measure the temperature of the snow to figure out what temperature wax to put on their skis. So if you are starting to get the idea that waxing can be a complicated affair, you're right. But we can leave all the complicated stuff to the racers and other avid fans of classic stride. For our purposes we can make do with the dirtbag approach. One way to go, is to use one of the two wax systems that are out on the market. In general these systems have one can of wax for cold dry snow and one for warm wet snow. So all you have to do is figure out which type of snow is on the ground and off you go. Otherwise experiment with the different colored waxes to see which one gives you the stick you need, without being too sticky. Where I tend to ski—in Wyoming and Idaho—I have found that Special Purple or Extra Blue tend to work just great in a variety of conditions so that's pretty much all I use. When things warm up in the spring, I switch to a wet snow wax. If things get so warm that wax no longer works, I'll just start skinning up because klister is just to messy for my taste.

Applying wax to your skis is another one of those touchy areas. The downhill purists tend to always skin and would never be caught dead with any kick wax on the bottom of their skis. However, the flat-track crowd are usually armed with such an array of waxes, corks (used for smoothing out the wax and helping it bind to the ski) and methods of applications that you could write a book about it. I tend to think in terms of what will get me to the good skiing the fastest, so I enjoy using wax to quickly get into some of the back bowls because it lets me glide and ski down the smaller hills that the purists, with their skins on, will be shuffling down. At the same time, being a dirt bag, I don't like to bother with all those fancy techniques for waxing.

I tend to apply wax from about 10 inches in front of my binding to a few inches behind the heel of my boot. This is called the wax pocket. If I will be pulling a sled, I will make it longer. My method of applying wax to skis would clog the arteries of some Nordic skiers, but it works fine for me. I just take the can of wax and like a four-year-old with a crayon, rub it on the underside of my ski until it is all colored in. I used to then rub it or "cork" it in with my hand but lately I have stopped doing this out of laziness. Corking heats the wax up and helps it stick to the bottom of the ski longer. Experiment with a number of ways and waxes to come up with a system that you like. The biggest mistake I see beginning waxers make is not using enough wax. So if you find that your skis are slipping too much, try adding more wax or making a longer wax pocket. If this doesn't work then go to a warmer wax.

Now sometimes when I get to the top of a slope that I want to go down, I find I barely have any glide. In this case, either my ski partners are trying to restrain me so that they can get first tracks or my skis have iced up. The snow is sticking to the wax and won't come off easily. This common scenario is easy dealt with, however. The first thing I usually try is to stamp my foot down in a back and forth gliding motion to try and break the snow off. If this doesn't work, then I will scrape the bottom of my ski across my other ski. If this fails to work, try skiing across the top of someone else's ski to scrape off the snow. Clear this with the person beforehand, though, as some people are mighty picky about their ski tops. If you are still icing up, then you have gooped too much wax on for conditions, used too soft a wax or the snow temperature has changed. Now you will need to get out your handy-dandy scraper and scrape the wax off. With a metal scraper, be careful not to scrape off the P-tex base material on the bottom of your skis. A plastic one avoids this problem but takes longer. If you forgot the scraper, another ski edge will work in a pinch, but once again be careful not to damage the bases.

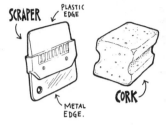

SCRAPER — PLASTIC EDGE

METAL EDGE.

CORK

OoOPS, WRONG WAX!

SCRAPE THE OTHER SKI BACK and FORTH TO CLEAN OFF the WAX pocket

TILT ONE SKI TO EXPOSE THE TOP EDGE

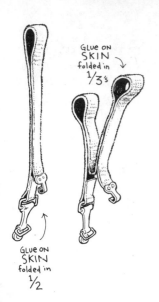

Glue on
SKIN
folded in
1/3's

GLUE ON
SKIN
folded in
1/2

Put the
RUBBER TIP
on First

SET the TAIL
on yer toe...

FLIP THE SKI OVER
and
attach the
tail clip...
SLIDE IT SIDEWAYS!

Some people like to scrape their wax off before they do a run anyway, but I find that if my wax is right I don't even notice it. As my wax ages on the bottom of my ski, I find that it tends to work better and better in a variety of conditions. Therefore, I don't tend to do a lot of scraping if I can help it nor do I add new wax to my skis very often.

SKINS

For people who abhor the idea of kick wax on the bottom of their skis, or for climbing those really steep long hills, skins are a mandatory part of a backcountry skiers quiver. Skins will allow you to climb virtually straight up most slopes or at least take a much steeper line then would be possible with wax. They will vastly increase your efficiency on long hill climbs and are worth their weight in gold. However skins do not glide across the snow like a wax, so they are less efficient for the flatter approaches. See page 24 for a description of the different types of skins.

The INCREDIBLE
Remove your skins with your
SKIS ON TECHNIQUE!

There is a definite crowd of skiers who would never let even a smidgen of kick wax touch their ski bases. They argue that wax doesn't work, slows them down too much on downhill runs and is unnecessary now that skins exist. This limited view comes from a lack of experience in using kick wax, I believe. Although sometimes I may be too much of a wax geek, I do believe there is a good compromise between waxing and skinning. A truly versatile backcountry skier will use a wax on those long flat approaches to maximize their glide, then make the switch to skins for yo-yoing the back bowls and getting in the maximum amount of downhill runs before making the long wax trip back out.

Remember... those shorty poles are a real bummer for traveling!

Nice & Long!

always plant your pole angled back, ready for pushin'!

Another argument against putting wax on skis is that it is a pain to scrape off and gunk's up the glue on the skins if you don't scrape it. A simple way to solve this is just not worry about it. My friend Mark convinced me long ago that it isn't necessary to clean off the bases. He just slaps the skins on over the wax and lets 'em gum up. It doesn't decrease the skins performance at all or the frequency with which he reglues them. For others, the pain of scraping is out weighed by the effort saved waxing in the first place.

FLAT TRACK AND UPHILL TECHNIQUE

In the backcountry, we need to be able to move around efficiently or we just waste energy. Part of our efficiency comes in the way we travel. Skiing in the backcountry is not all about

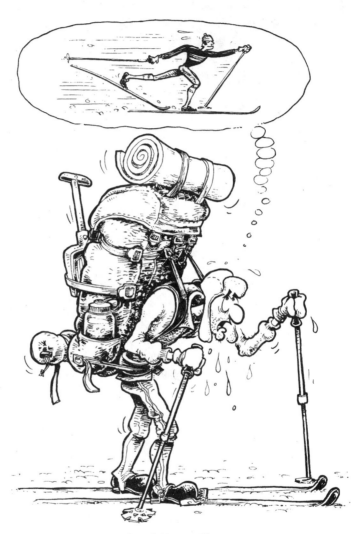

DON'T EXPECT TO
DO MUCH MORE THAN
PLOD ALONG
when you are
humping the
MONSTER LOAD!

going downhill; it also involves going uphill and moving across flat terrain. With the heavier gear we use for downhill skiing we should not expect to look like those classic Nordic stride racers, especially if we are skiing with a heavy pack, but neither do we need to slog along like a snowshoer. Skis are wonderful, that magical ability to glide across the snows surface makes skiing an amazingly fun and efficient way to travel.

KICK AND GLIDE

We probably ought to call this "the shuffle" since realistically this is more or less what you will be doing. However adding some kick and glide to your travel at times will definitely get you moving a little faster. Remember when shifting your weight from one ski to another, shift all your weight not just part of it. When going uphill you should shorten your stride and really punch down with your heel to get maximum stick. The biggest mistake people make when trying to climb hills is leaning too far forward. This puts your weight over the front of the skis instead of the middle, where you want it. So really think about standing up ramrod straight and taking short steps with your heels punching down into the snow. Use your poles but don't rely on them to push you up the hill.

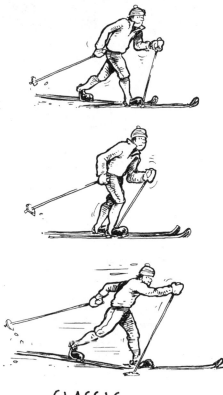

CLASSIC KICK and GLIDE

Transfer all your weight from foot to foot as you push off each ski. Opposite arm reaches forward with the opposing foot, just like you naturally do walking.

Get full power and extension from each kick. Arms out reaching down the track.

DOUBLE-POLING

This technique works well if you have some speed or a glide on a downhill. Lean forward and plant both poles in front of you.

Bend at the waist and push off the poles with the arms and abdominals for the most power.

DOUBLE-POLE KICK and GLIDE

Another technique for increasing the amount of speed and glide on the flats slight downhills. Reach forward with b poles and as you kick forward onto yo other ski do a double pole plant. Once again your power and endurance here enhanced by bringing the abdominals into play.

TURNING

Kick turns are what most people think about here. The biggest mistake I see in people doing a kick-turn is not keeping their skis perpendicular to the fall line. This invariably leads to one of the skis slipping out from underneath them. Other methods of turning on flat ground involve any number of pick your ski up and put it back down (in a different orientation) combinations.

THE ALL IMPORTANT KICK TURN:
① First, you'll need a pole behind you or you'll kick it. ② Lift that ski and... ③ Swing it around with one bold (and smooth) movement. ④ Next, bring that other pole around, but plant it a bit off to one side. ⑤ Now... bring that second ski around, but don't hit that pole! ⑥ Finally, re-position that pole & yer done!

ROLL YOUR KNEES INWARD!

inside edges IN!

HERRINGBONE

The important thing in the herringbone is to get those edges into the snow. Otherwise, you may just find your self sliding back down. This technique is mostly useful for climbing short packed slopes of moderate steepness and is very hard to pull off in deep powder.

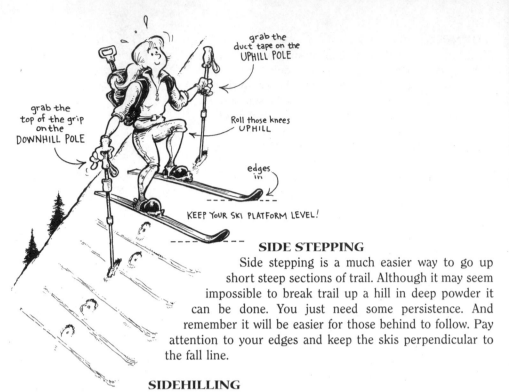

grab the
duct tape on the
UPHILL POLE

grab the
top of the grip
on the
DOWNHILL POLE

Roll those knees
UPHILL

edges
in

KEEP YOUR SKI PLATFORM LEVEL!

SIDE STEPPING

Side stepping is a much easier way to go up short steep sections of trail. Although it may seem impossible to break trail up a hill in deep powder it can be done. You just need some persistence. And remember it will be easier for those behind to follow. Pay attention to your edges and keep the skis perpendicular to the fall line.

SIDEHILLING

This is the most useful technique for climbing those long hills or short hills where your direction is not limited by the terrain. I think of sidehilling or traversing as a combination of forward moving side steps that can be combined with kick turns at the end of a traverse (see switchbacks, page 58). With skins on or by using a low-angled track you can avoid side stepping and break or follow the trail using just a shortened stride.

BREAKING TRAIL

There comes a time when we've all got to break trail in the backcountry. For some, this is a daunting task they would like to see end as soon as possible. Others find it an enjoyable and challenging part of being in the backcountry. I personally enjoy being in the front, finding my way through the untracked snow, picking the route through the trees

THIS IS HARD!

This is easy...

Breaking and Following
Trail

the DOWNHILL turn:

You keep a nice
balance with your
uphill pole... and
you don't need to
lift your skis too high
by turning away
from the uphill slope

the UPHILL turn:

Tricky Balancing!
You'll really need to hike
that ski high to
clear the uphill slope...
watch your pole when
you swing around!

a nice kick-turn
PLATFORM

and up the hills and breaking the trail for those behind. Think of it as the freedom from being stuck in the rut. So give it a try, because I believe once you get the hang of it you will find it enjoyable.

Some hints about breaking trail: On hard snow or when the new snow depth is so shallow that you stay close to the surface of the snow, it is not much extra work breaking trail. This is a good time to get up front and practice route finding. Once the snow starts getting deeper and/or heavier, the trial breaking becomes harder. You need to free your ski from under the snow with each step to avoid getting bogged down. Kick and pull your ski up and back until it breaks free. Leaning back as you do this will also add your body weight to the process of levering the ski tip free.

In deep snow conditions it is nice to have a relay. The relay gives the front person a chance to rest and speeds up the overall process of breaking trail because the person breaking trail can throw more energy into it when he or she knows that he or she will get some relief. The way relays work is that the front person breaks until he or she feels him- or herself slowing down or getting too hot. The front person then steps off the trail and rejoins at the back of the line. The next person takes over and the process is repeated. This way everyone cycles through and gets a chance to break trail. Another approach that works well when carrying heavy packs, the group is big and the trail-breaking hard is to have a couple people drop packs and break for 15 to 30 minutes. They then ski back to their packs and some others take over the trail-breaking. This way everyone takes a turn at breaking trail and everyone gets a break. The trail-breaking goes faster because the breakers are unencumbered, and it's easy to catch up with a well-packed trail.

SWITCHBACKS

Breaking trail up steeper hills often requires the use of switchbacks, especially if you are using wax. I like to wax if the hills are short but will put in a skin track if it promises to be a long climb. Typically when people do a skin track, they try to avoid kick turns because they are slower than just making a smooth round turn while stepping your skis forward. Also, if you are pulling a sled it is easier to do an uphill step turn than a kick turn.

There are two ways of doing kick turns on a hill, uphill and downhill. The advantage to turning uphill is that you don't lose any elevation executing the turn and it is faster once you get the hang of it. However, it is easier to get your skis hung up in the snow in front of you, and if you happen to fall over during the turn, Murphy's law says that you will fall backwards down the hill. A downhill kick turn is definitely the way to go on a steep hill and if you are carrying a heavy pack, but it is impossible with a sled.

One last thing on breaking trail is you should always break to your weakest group member in terms of skins, wax or ability. Otherwise the person winds up having to break his or her own trail. A waste of effort on both parts.

— PLEASE NOTE: —

this illustration clearly shows the various uphill methods...

BUT!

IF I EVER CATCH A CROWD OF GUMBIES TRASHIN' A PERFECT POWDER RUN with a bunch of uphill tracks first they'd catch an earful, then I'd impale 'em all with my pointy probe poles!

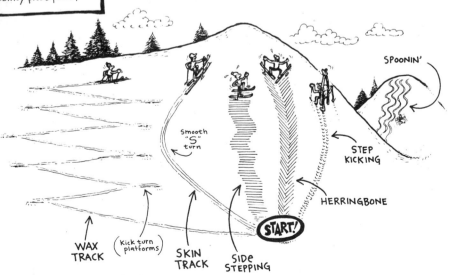

SPOONIN'

Smooth "S" turn

STEP KICKING

HERRINGBONE

START!

WAX TRACK

(kick turn platforms)

SKIN TRACK

SIDE STEPPING

CAMPING IN THE SNOW

KEEP MEALS WARM!

LID

YUMMY

SPOON

A PLASTIC BOWL
for EATING,
INSULATED with some
ENSOLITE foam WRAPPED
with DUCT-TAPE!

If you want to go camping at a time when the hordes of people and bugs are at their absolute minimum, winter is the time to go. Of course, this is not the only advantage. It is also a wonderful time to be out. Travel over the snow is easy, elaborate camps can be built with little impact on the land and the beauty of being out on a clear moonlight night can't be beat. All this, plus the fact that by going just a few miles into the mountains, you'll discover gigantic areas of untracked snow waiting for you to ski.

SNOW KITCHENS

One of the best things about winter camping is what you can to do with your shovel, some effort and vision. You can build very comfortable camps out of snow. In the following chapter,

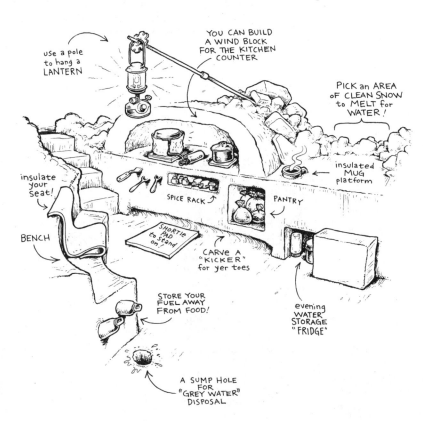

use a pole to hang a LANTERN

YOU CAN BUILD A WIND BLOCK FOR THE KITCHEN COUNTER

PICK an AREA oF CLEAN SNOW to MELT for WATER!

insulated MUG platform

insulate your seat!

SPICE RACK

PANTRY

BENCH

SHORTIE PAD to stand on!

CARVE A "KICKER" for yer toes

STORE YOUR FUEL AWAY FROM FOOD!

evening WATER STORAGE "FRIDGE"

A SUMP HOLE FOR "GREY WATER" DISPOSAL

INSULATOR
made with closed cell foam
and DUCT TAPE

KEEP yer ENERGY BARS
WARM by PACKING 'em
into an insulated
H_2O BOTTLE COVER.

use a polar bootie
to keep your
WATER BOTTLE from
freezing.

GAG!

BURNT SNOW!

we will talk about snow shelters but even if you are out with a tent a snow kitchen can be an object of beauty and function.

By piling snow up and digging down, you can make counters, tabletops and seats. I have even made alcoves and half-open snow caves to cook in during nasty weather. It is important to remember that if you want a covered kitchen it needs to be well ventilated. Carbon monoxide fumes from stoves or lanterns are impossible to detect and deadly.

When building with snow, work hardening is imperative. Packing down the snow with shovels, skis or boots makes it denser and harder. You have probably experienced this before making snowballs or shoveling snow that has been plowed. So if your snow is too soft for counters or seats, stomp on it for awhile and give it some time to set up before shaving things into the shape you want them. Experiment, experiment, experiment to figure out what works and what you like the best. Shoveling is a part of the winter experience, and I like to think of it as another way to get in shape.

I try to find an east-facing spot for my kitchens whenever possible. Mornings are typically the coldest part of the day, and this helps ensure the sun will arrive at the earliest possible moment. Once you have your kitchen area picked out, it is important not to contaminate the snow around it. This is where you will be getting your snow for melting into water. It is a good idea to designate other areas for urination.

One of the drawbacks of winter camping is the sudden onset of darkness in the early evening. This is easily overcome by bringing along a few candles and maybe even a lantern. Candles placed in a clear plastic bag or well protected from the wind in a kitchen alcove will provide sufficient light for cooking and other such activities. A small lantern will provide an amazing amount of light off the highly reflective snow and is a definite plus for those lush winter trips.

THE WHYS AND HOWS OF COOKING AND MELTING SNOW

Besides the three Ss of winter camping (skiing, shoveling and sleeping) cooking and melting snow will be the next most time-consuming activities. Eating is important for maintaining your energy and staying warm. You can think of it as the fuel for your engine. Water is the oil, and you need plenty of it in the cold and dry winter air. Drinking four quarts of water a day wouldn't be overding it.

MAKING WATER

Melting snow for water can be a time- and fuel-consuming process. But unless you happen to be camped near open water it is necessary. Be aware that you can scorch the snow. I know this sounds ridiculous to the uninitiated, but it is entirely possible to have your water taste like burnt rice. Believe it or not I first experienced this phenomenon in the high deserts of Utah. There we were camped in the snow with no water in sight. So we threw some snow in our pot and stuck it on the stove and wha-la, lousy-tasting burnt water is what we got.

The easiest way to avoid this undesirable result is to place some water in the pot with the snow. This keeps the pot from scorching the snow. If you have no water then starting with a small amount of snow in the pot and stirring rapidly until you get some water is the next best solution. If you don't believe me about scorching the water then give it a try with some dry snow. Bon appetit.

If you happen to be camping near open water, you're in luck. You won't need to spend as much time around the roar of the stove. Two things to keep in mind are access to the water and its purification. Make sure you can get to the water source without falling in. The only thing worse then getting your feet wet is going for a swim. The need to treat water for giardia and other waterborne illnesses is the same as it is in the summer. It will take about twice as long for chemicals purifiers, such as iodine, to work but they won't freeze like a water filter will. I like to use Potable Aqua as it is light and small. Bringing the water to a boil also works just fine.

STORING WATER

You decide to make a pot of water the night before so you can get an early jump on the skiing in the morning, but when you get up, you discover that what you have in the morning is a pot of ice. Bummer. You can avoid this troubling scenario by actually burying your water in the snow!

IF YOU HAVE IT! add a little water to the pot...

At first, add snow SLOWLY and STIR!

Once you get some liquid in the bottom, add some bigger chunks...

Keep the lid on when you ain't adding snow!

HEY! There's snow stuck to your pot!

CAREFUL! that snow'll put out the stove!

The incredible little pot pad!

FUEL
For melting snow, cooking and lanterns a liter of white gas a day per three people seems to be about right. This can be fine-tuned according to your stove and how efficiently you cook. Butane users should take at least three times the amount of fuel they would normally take in the summer.

evening
WATER
STORAGE:
make a "drawer"
in the kitchen
for all your water.

keep the water bottles
upside-down so the
lids don't freeze!

use a snow block
for a little
refridgerator door!

DRINK the
PASTA WATER
YOU MELTED THAT SNOW,
DON'T WASTE IT!

always
KEEP
YOUR MUG
from
TIPPING

SPICE
IT UP

HOT.   SOY.   MISO.

Snow is an excellent insulator. This is one of the reasons animals dig into the snow to sleep. We can use this insulation to our advantage. By placing a pot of water down a hole in the snow and then covering it with a block of snow or some bags, you can keep it from freezing into a solid block of ice. Then in the morning you have water to start the day with and won't have to spend those precious daylight hours melting snow.

I like to go to bed with at least 2 quarts of water per person already made. What you want ideally is to have enough water made so that when you get up you can have one or two hot drinks, breakfast and full water bottles for the day's activities without having to melt a whole bunch of snow.

EATING

Food is a good thing. Anyone who spends a great deal of time winter camping is sure to agree. In the winter, where we are the main source of heat, we need lots of calories to stay warm and active. A good mark to shoot for is 3,700 to 4,500 calories per day. This equates to about 2 to 2.5 pounds of dry food per person per day. The NOLS Cookery is an excellent source of informa-

TIPS
Some people like to drink their pasta water as a hot drink to save time and fuel for melting water. Proper spicing is essential to make it palatable.

To speed up the process of turning snow into water, think about bringing a second stove—especially if you are in a group of three or more.

SEARCHING for some running WATER...

tion and recipes for those about to embark on any wilderness adventure. Whatever you do, don't short yourself on food in the winter because it is a very unpleasant time to be hungry and cold.

Foods high in fats, such as cheese and nuts, will supply about twice the calories per gram as other types of food. Whereas carbohydrates provide about 4 calories per gram, fat provides over 8. It also takes longer for our bodies to digest fats. What does this mean for us in the winter environment? If we eat a dinner of macaroni and cheese versus just macaroni then we get more calories that will last longer, therefore we will stay warmer as we sleep the night away. On the other side of the coin, eating cheese or nuts to give us some energy for that long hill climb just ahead won't really work. By the time we actually metabolize and start getting energy from these types of food, the hill climb will long be over. Thus for trail snacks it is better to eat more simple carbos like crackers, dried fruit and chocolate. In the end it is wise to eat some fats and lots of carbos throughout the day . This will give us the short- and long-term energy we need to keep ourselves going.

TIPS

Precut cheese and meats into small squares before going out, otherwise they will freeze into a solid block that you will need a chain saw to cut.

Candy and other such wrappers are hard to deal with in the wintertime as they tend to blow away or get lost. Just try to unwrap one with mittens on and not litter the world. Unwrapping and bulk bagging food before you go is an easier way to deal with it in the winter.

Get rid of food boxes and excess packaging, i.e., crackers and cookies, by rebagging these items as well.

A dish with a screw-on lid for butter or margarine works well and protects your pack from a grease attack.

Frozen oil or liquid in plastic jars can be thawed by placing it in hot water.

Your menu can also include frozen vegetables and meats. Your fridge at home could be warmer than your campsite!

TIPS FOR LIGHTING A STOVE IN COLD WEATHER

In cold weather stove fuel (both butane and white gas) can be hard to light initially, especially after a night of extremely cold temperatures. You can keep the fuel in the tent or snow shelter to keep it warmer or warm it under your parka before using.

With white gas, you can hold a lighter or match flame to the gas in the spirit cup until it heats up enough to ignite. Also try preheating the spirit cup with a lighter before adding the gas to it.

I w-w-w-WANT!

BUTTER!

HOT CHOCOLATE!

I-80 TRUCK STOP

ON LONGER EXPEDITIONS YOUR BODY WILL BE CRAVING MASSIVE CALORIES...

(THIS MEANS FAT!)

Bon Appétit!

OOOOOH!

AHHHH!

YOU CAN USE A SMALL WATER BOTTLE FOR HOT DRINKS!

this makes for a nice hand warmer...

OR BETTER YET... stick that BOTTLE full of HOT DRINK IN YOUR COAT near your body!

Can't do that with a mug!

Variety is the spice of life so don't limit yourself to just power bars, which can be dangerous to your dental work anyway if you don't warm them up.

When cooking remember to pick up food scraps as you go along. I like to keep a small bag for garbage handy just to make it easier. Leaving food behind makes for sloppy camps and encourages animals to think of us as soup kitchens. I personally hate it when the wildlife starts demanding that I feed it, especially when it is bigger than me, so I appreciate it when we clean up after ourselves.

CAREFUL
WITH those FROZEN
ROCK HARD TREATS!

CAREFUL! Not everything freezes solid!

CLEANLINESS

An important part of staying healthy and of camping in good style is the degree to which you clean. There is nothing more disgusting in my mind than cooking meal after meal in the same dirty pot. I mean it really doesn't take much effort or time to clean a pot with some warm water or snow. Then you have a nice clean pot for the next meal. In addition, you lessen the risk of

> **CAREFUL!**
> **Liquids that don't freeze at low temperatures, such as alcohol and white gas, can cause frostbite damage because they will be the same temperature as the air.**

contracting some foodborne illness. Dry scrape the pot first with a spoon or spatula to get out all the big food scraps and put them in your garbage. With the rest it is best to sump it in one spot as this avoids contaminating the snow/water source. Also keep your hands clean for cooking. If you have a special pair of thin gloves for cooking with, you lessen the chance of passing on germs and it helps keep your hands warmer. It is also a good idea to wash your hands (before cooking and after pooping) with some warm water if they are really dirty.

TIME TO
WAKE UP...
OATMEAL'S
READY!

REMEMBER
PROPER HYGIENE
in the kitchen

Tight fitting lid!

LABEL IT!

use a textured bottle so you don't confuse it with your water bottle!

Women's PEE-TUB

tight fitting lid!

foot position for proper use

the ALL important
PEE BOTTLES

SLEEPING WARM

Eating and drinking enough is critical to sleeping warm. A big dinner with lots of calories can really get your metabolism going. If you find that you wake up cold during the late hours of the night, take a little food to bed to help replenish lost calories and get your metabolism going again. The same goes for water. Being dehydrated is the cause for so many ailments, it is surprising we don't hear more about it in everyday life. The flip side however, is being over hydrated. It is no fun having to get up ten times during the night to pee. One to three time a night is plenty. Voiding our bladders is important for staying warm, though. If you are holding it in, your body will be wasting energy keeping all that water at 98.6 degrees. By peeing we have more energy to spare for ourselves and we will be more comfortable. I often use a pee bottle in the winter, but unfortunately this option does not work for us all. In any case, getting up during the night affords us the opportunity to check out the weather and is beneficial to our sleep in the long run.

The first thing you should do before climbing in your sleeping bag at night is to get nice and warm. Go for a ski or post hole your way around camp once or twice. I prefer to do a bunch of last minute shovel work on the kitchen. Whatever you do, your goal is to get toasty warm. A sleeping bag can be thought of like a Thermos: If you put something warm in it, it keeps it warm. If you put something cold in, it stays cold. So go to bed warm.

I also like to sleep in most of my insulating layers. Heck, once I even slept with my boots on. This way you don't have to take all that time getting dressed and undressed. Plus it's easier to get out of bed if you are already dressed in warm clothes. All this hype about sleeping bare naked just sounds cold to me. Of course if you wear clothes that are so tight as to be constric-

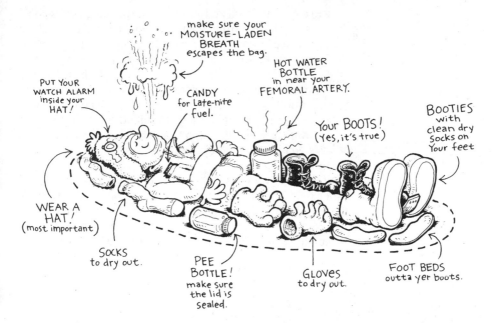

make sure your MOISTURE-LADEN BREATH escapes the bag.

PUT YOUR WATCH ALARM inside your HAT!

CANDY for Late-nite fuel.

HOT WATER BOTTLE in near your FEMORAL ARTERY.

Your BOOTS! (Yes, it's true)

BOOTIES with clean dry socks on your feet

WEAR A HAT! (most important)

SOCKS to dry out.

PEE BOTTLE! make sure the lid is sealed.

GLOVES to dry out.

FOOT BEDS outta yer boots.

tive, then perhaps you should take them off—or go buy some larger clothes. A hat is also a wonderful thing to wear to bed. People always underestimate the importance of keeping your head warm. If you find that you are sleeping too warm then take the hat off and/or try unzipping the bag before taking off layers.

My friend Tom always had trouble with cold feet during the night. No matter how many loose socks or booties he slept with his feet were always cold. I suggested that instead of wrapping his feet up separately at night, he try wrapping them together in a pile jacket with just a single pair of socks on. I theorized that then his feet would be able to share heat instead of being isolated. Luckily for the two of us it worked! He had warm feet and I had credibility.

Sleeping pads are important for a warm night's sleep. The two coldest nights I ever had were when I didn't even own a pad, and one night when I rolled off my pad. I couldn't figure out why I was so cold until I woke up in the morning to find that I had rolled about 10 feet from where my ensolite was. We lose an incredible amount of heat to the snow via conduction so the more we can protect against this the cozier we will be. I personally like to have at least two full length ensolite pads or a thermarest and an ensolite. If you have a synthetic parka and pants, you can also place these between your bag and the pads for more insulation.

If after all this you find that you are still cold, you have two options left. One is to try snuggling closer to your campmates.

this is LITTER!

ENSOLITE FOAM PAD carried on the outside of your pack showing BUSHWACKING DAMAGE!

USE A STUFF SACK OR... PUT IT INSIDE YER PACK!

Even if you don't zip together, just spooning allows you to suck therms from them and possibly tip that balance between cold and warm. I personally highly recommend therm sucking. The other option, not quite as friendly, is to take a hot water bottle to bed. The heat from this can be strategically placed at any cold spots until they are warmed up. You will also then have warm water to sip on during the night. Warning for those with pee bottles! Don't get the two mixed up unless you like rude awakenings.

UNDER THE STARS

From time to time I enjoy sleeping out under the stars. Its great to wake up at night and see the sky overhead. It also makes for lots of elbow room getting up and going to bed, and if you have smelly tent mates, well.... However, it is definitely a

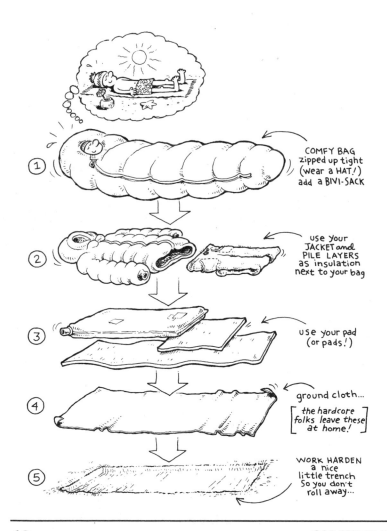

① COMFY BAG zipped up tight (wear a HAT!) add a BIVI-SACK

② use your JACKET and PILE LAYERS as insulation next to your bag

③ use your pad (or pads!)

④ ground cloth... [the hardcore folks leave these at home!]

⑤ WORK HARDEN a nice little trench so you don't roll away...

lot colder sleeping out because you radiate heat into space instead of trapping it in the walls around you.

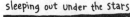

Using a bivy bag can help add another 10 degrees or so to your sleeping bag. Sleeping underneath a tree, while blocking your view of the stars, saves a significant amount of heat loss through radiation as well. I have even weathered out storms by sleeping under the thick canopy of spruce trees. Although sleeping out in the winter isn't for everyone, some folks find it very enjoyable and not all of them are claustrophobic.

FIRES FOR EMERGENCIES

In the winter it is not easy to find wood lying around. This is one reason why fires are generally not appropriate for winter. Another reason is the difficulty of building a fire on top of the snow. There are times, however, when some type of emergency may dictate a fire to keep folks warm or to rewarm a hypothermic patient. At these times, it is important to know how to get one going in the snow.

HEAT RADIATES AWAY!

First, you need to know where to gather wood. Using live trees is a poor option as green wood does not burn readily. I look for dead trees that have fallen over and have branches sticking up above the snow. These can be easily collected along with other dead branches from still living trees. A good place to find small branches for kindling is low down on the dead branches of spruce trees, since these are dry and burn well.

Once you have gathered the wood take the largest pieces and lay them on the snow. These will form the platform on which to build the fire. Now using the kindling and any fire starter you have, pile it on your platform and light it. If you have no fire starter then make wood shavings with a knife. You can use a stove or the gas from a stove to get things going as well but be careful since gas is a very volatile substance. If you lack these things then using the absolute smallest pieces of kindling you can find should work. If you don't have a lighter or matches, you're out of luck and you should think about what it means to be prepared.

sleeping under a tree
REFLECTS SOME HEAT BACK

The platform you build should keep the fire up off the snow, so it doesn't go out. If you have ever read anything by Jack London, you know to be wary of lighting the fire underneath a tree loaded with snow as well. When it is going strong you can use a space blanket to reflect the heat behind you. If you brought a tin can or pots then you can also make hot water. Be careful about setting all those nylon clothes on fire.

USE STICKS
about the thickness
of a pencil

work harden
SNOW
SURFACE

PLATFORM

SEW a POCKET
onto your base
LAYER OF UNDERWEAR!
this is an invaluable
place to keep stuff
that'd be useless
FROZEN SOLID!

ZIPPER
PULL
made from
some
STRING!

KEEPING IT SIMPLE

Winter camping is a fun and challenging way to experience the winter. But not everything will work the same for every person, and for this reason it is a good idea to start out slow. Start off close to the road so that you will have an easy bail out if things aren't going right. Experiment with different techniques and find out what works for you. Make things as simple as possible; it will increase efficiency and reduce frustration. An example of making things simple is putting zipper pulls on everything so you can zip with mittens on.

I'm not a fan of lots of little storage pockets. I can never remember where I put something, and it is far easier for me to search in one big place then in a bunch of small pockets or stuff sacks. Trying to pack everything into its own little sack also makes packing up a long drawn out affair. Nothing ever fits as easily as it did in town, and the act of stuffing nylon sleeping bags, bivy bags, sleeping pads, tents, extra clothes and so on in their own little bags just makes my hands cold. Instead I like to have a lightweight medium-sized duffel bag for my extra clothes and stuff I don't need while on the trail. (Mike uses a huge nylon laundry bag.) This bag, and other things like my sleeping bag, gets shoved into the bottomless pit of my pack. I keep my extra layers, food and water for the trail on top of all this. Then when I stop, all I have to do is open up the top of my pack and everything that I need for a break is there. In the very top pouch of my pack is where I keep all the little stuff like sunglasses, sunscreen, waxes and skins. If I am using side pockets, I will put miscellaneous stuff like repair kits, fuel bottles, probes, snow saws, etc., in them.

When I use a sled, I have my pack filled with all the stuff I need for the day, and the sled is packed with all the stuff I need in camp. This way I can ski around without the sled and not worry about having left anything behind.

DRESSING FOR THE WINTER

Nothing is more important to your comfort and health than dressing properly for the winter environment. I once experienced a –40 degrees day in February only to have it warm up to just below freezing later in the day. In the morning I was wearing everything I had to stay warm while cooking breakfast,

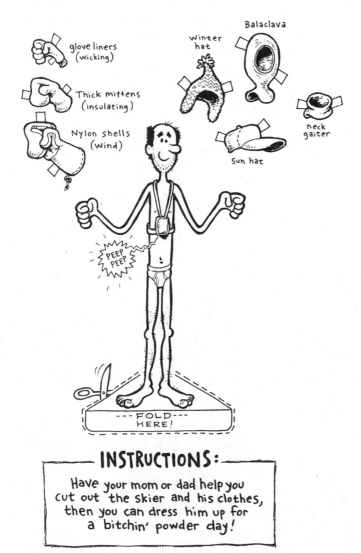

glove liners
(wicking)

Thick mittens
(insulating)

Nylon shells
(Wind)

Winter
hat

Balaclava

neck
gaiter

Sun hat

PEEP
PEEP

---FOLD---
HERE!

INSTRUCTIONS:

Have your mom or dad help you cut out the skier and his clothes, then you can dress him up for a bitchin' powder day!

Wicking underwear Layer

and in the afternoon I was breaking trail in nothing but light-weight poly pro. For this reason, the use of multiple layers in the winter is the way to go. This gives you the option of wearing enough clothes to stay warm, but not so many that you will sweat to death while performing physical activities.

SOME IDEAS ABOUT LAYERING

Cotton clothing is not a good idea in the winter. The problem with cotton is that when it gets wet from sweating or falling down in the snow, it has no insulating value and takes forever to dry. Wearing a wet cotton shirt next to your body is not only uncomfortable but potentially dangerous to your health as well. So nix the cotton.

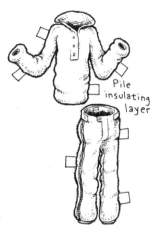

Pile insulating layer

Clothes made of wool or synthetic materials, such as polypropylene, capilene, Dacron, etc., are the way to go in the winter. Not only do they retain insulating properties when wet, but many of the synthetics help to wick moisture away from the body keeping you drier. Synthetic materials will dry quicker and easier than wool and are usually lighter, although they are less eco-groovy.

A distinction is made between wicking and insulating layers. In general wicking layers are meant to be worn close to the skin, as the material in them is designed to help draw water away from your skin. Polypropylene is a good example of this. Insulating layers may also dry quickly depending on the mate-

Fancy and Expensive Wind Layer.

Light Nylon Wind Layer.

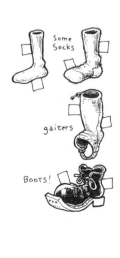

Some Socks

gaiters

Boots!

SPIN YOUR ARM
to warm your
FINGERS and HAND

SWING yer LEGS
back and forth to
WARM yer FEET!

rial used, but are mainly designed to trap dead air space and slow the loss of body heat. Pile, wool, Quallofil and down are examples of some of the materials used for insulation.

Wind/snow shedding layers are also important. These slick outer layers of nylon help block the wind from stealing your heat and keep you from looking like the abominable snowman. Your layers should strip off easily or vent well since nothing is worse than climbing a hill with too many layers on.

A TOURING OUTFIT

Here are some ideas on what to bring for a day of touring in the backcountry. These same layers will also form the basic layers for overnight trips into the mountains. The best way to figure out what works is to experiment on your various trips. Eventually you will come up with a system you like. It is important to be prepared for any eventuality, however. So if you never have experienced any really cold weather, you shouldn't assume you won't. You need to carry enough to deal with possible situations such as colder than normal temperatures or an unplanned bivouac. I always carry an extra layer in my pack for that one eventuality when I need it.

Most of my experience is in the intermountain west and my suggestions reflect this. If I was doing a trip in the Pacific Northwest or the Northeast, I might do some things differently. Having a rain coat in my pack is one example. Typically I don't bring a rain coat winter camping in Wyoming. But if I went to

> **TIPS FOR WARM HANDS AND FEET**
>
> **Prewarm your boots in the morning with a small pint-sized hot water bottle. Warm up your socks on your shoulders.**
>
> **Stay active and warm; a cold core means cold extremities so by keeping your core warm you make it easier to warm up your extremities.**
>
> **By aggressively swinging your arms and legs you can force warm blood to flow into them.**
>
> **You can rewarm any extremity by placing it on some else's warm belly. This can be key in preventing frost bite.**
>
> **Stay hydrated; dehydration leads to sluggish circulation and thus cold hands and feet.**

How to use a
VAPOR BARRIER LINER
system

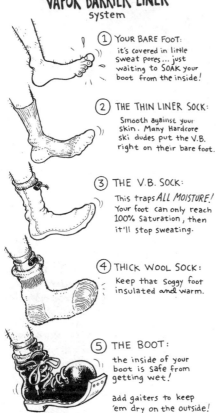

(1) YOUR BARE FOOT:
it's covered in little
sweat pores... just
waiting to SOAK your
boot from the inside!

(2) THE THIN LINER SOCK:
Smooth against your
skin. Many Hardcore
ski dudes put the V.B.
right on their bare foot.

(3) THE V.B. SOCK:
This traps *ALL MOISTURE!*
Your foot can only reach
100% Saturation, then
it'll stop sweating.

(4) THICK WOOL SOCK:
Keep that soggy foot
insulated and warm.

(5) THE BOOT:
the inside of your
boot is safe from
getting wet!

add gaiters to keep
'em dry on the outside!

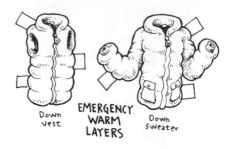

EMERGENCY
WARM
LAYERS
Down Vest   Down Sweater

another **V.B. fact.**

YOUR FEET'LL
STINK... BAD!

and
they'll be
PRUNEY!

the Sierras, with its wetter conditions, I would bring one. The time of year can make a difference as well. In the spring you are less likely to experience extremely cold weather but more likely to get rained upon.

For upper body layers I like to wear medium and expedition weight synthetics and a wind shirt. I personally like a wind shirt made of nylon and not GoreTex since it is lighter and more breathable and packs away smaller. However, there are a lot of skiers out there who swear by their GoreTex jackets. I also carry a warm jacket and a vest in my pack for putting on during breaks and for emergencies. If it is really cold, I bring along an additional insulating layer. When breaking trail I often have on just my lightest layer; then again, sometimes when skiing down a hill on a cold windy day, I have on all my layers. This is the beauty of a layered system.

On my lower body I wear the equivalent of expedition or heavyweight poly pro. In reality this is a lightweight poly pro bottom covered with some cheapo nylon sweat pants. I hide this fact under some lightweight wind pants that I got out of a lost-and-never-found box or some tacky thrift store. If I am lucky enough to have full-length side zips on my wind pants, then on really sunny days I can zip them off for long trail climbs. If not, no big deal. This system has worked so well for me that I can't imagine giving it up. On the other hand, most of the people I ski with cover up their poly pro or wool pants with GoreTex bibs. These have the definite advantage of limiting the amount of snow that goes up the back when you fall. And since they all have long side zips, they are easy to ventilate.

do-it-your-self
CHEAP-O
V.B. LINeRS!

PLASTIC PRODUCE
bags from the
Grocery store
work fine.

They'll break,
so take a
clean pair
for every
day or so...

CAMPING IN THE SNOW

For the head, hands and feet I like to wear a hat, mittens and socks. Seriously though, you shouldn't underestimate the value of a warm hat. The head contains lots of blood vessels and can be a huge source of heat loss, so insulating it from the elements does far more than just keep the forehead warm. Some people like balaclavas, others ski hats and neck gaiters and still others a combination of the two. As long as its functional and warm, it doesn't matter. I like a warm hat that is covered with nylon to keep the snow off. For warmer days I bring a wool headband to keep my ears warm when I'm not wearing my hat.

I prefer mittens to gloves as they keep my fingers warmer. They should fit comfortably over a pair of thin liner gloves for doing those things you just can't do with mitts. I like these knitted nylon gloves from Well Lamont, which cost a little over a dollar at most grocery stores. But any wool or synthetic gloves will do. With any mittens, you should also get some mitten shells to keep the snow off. An advantage to the mitten shell combo is you can just wear the shell with thin gloves on those really warm days.

As for socks, I'm a firm believer in wearing two heavy pairs with your boots for warmth. I'm not a fan of vapor barrier liners since they make my feet wet and cold, but there are plenty of people who like them. They do keep your socks and boots dry from sweat on multiday trips. Remember that you need to be careful and diligent about getting out of those soggy VBL's and changing into your booty system when you get into camp at the end of the day.

CAMP CLOTHES

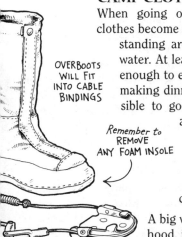

OVERBOOTS WILL FIT INTO CABLE BINDINGS

Remember to REMOVE ANY FOAM INSOLE

You'll need to Loosen the Bindings a little

When going out on an extended trip more clothes become necessary for those tasks such as standing around at night melting snow for water. At least if you want to be comfortable enough to enjoy sitting out doing things like making dinner, reading stories, etc. It is possible to go lighter, but this requires more activity to stay warm and earlier nights to bed. I will cover clothing options that err toward the comfortable side and you can eliminate what you want, but be careful, it can get cold out there.

A big warm parka, especially one with a hood, is key to staying warm. Synthetic or down is a question that gets asked. I think it depends on where you live and ski—and on your pocketbook. I have

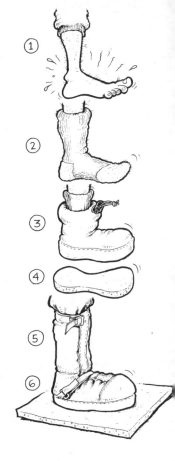

the BOOTY SYSTEM!

① Start with dry FEET, then add...

② one (or TWO) pairs of DRY SOCKS...

③ POLY (or DOWN) BOOTIES...

④ ENSOLITE FOOT BEDS, or even better, TWO of 'em taped together, in the bottom of yer...

⑤ OVER-BOOTS!

⑥ SHORTIE PAD! stand on it...

FULL ON
WINTER
CAMP
ensemble

HOT
CHOCOLATE!

Shortie
Pad!

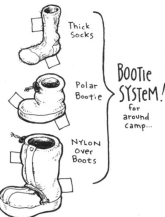

Thick
Socks

**BOOTie
SYSTeM!**
for
around
camp...

Polar
Bootie

NYLON
over
Boots

insulating
camp
Layers

used both successfully. Down is light, warm and packs small, but it is expensive and the downy feathers lose all their insulating properties when soaked with water and become just one heavy glob. Synthetics are getting to be more like down (including the price) but still function when wet. This is a definite advantage in wetter climates. Along with the parka, a pair of insulated pants are very nice, especially if you are prone to cold feet.

Since it is nice to get out of your boots after a long day of skiing, having some type of booty system is key. To prevent cold injuries such as immersion foot it is important to change into dry socks once you make camp. This is especially true if your feet are cold and damp. Once in camp I like to change into a pair of dry socks, and slip my feet into some down socks, a pair of booties with an insulated bottom, and finally into some overboots with ensolite insoles for even greater insulation. If I am skiing with double boots and supergaiters, I take the liners out of them and wear the outer boot as my overboots. The important thing here is that you have something that is knee high to keep the snow out when walking around in deep snow. Now what about those damp socks you have just taken off? Read on.

STAYING DRY AND DRYING OUT

Getting wet is the bane of backcountry skiers. Although it is not as horrible when you are just out for a day tour, it makes for a miserable and dangerous experience if you are out overnight. But it happens and there are ways to dry out. Prevention is once again the key to staying dry. I try to avoid getting wet on overnights by limiting the number of times I fall into the snow while skiing and by wearing clothes that will shed snow. If I am doing lots of downhill skiing and find my clothes starting to get soaked from falling, then I call it a good day and head back to camp for some hot drinks. I also get damp from sweat when breaking trail on warm days. To limit how much I sweat and how many layers get wet, I strip off unneeded clothes. If it is really cold and I can't afford to be taking off layers, I go at a slower speed and pace myself so I don't sweat.

KEEP DAMP SOCKS and GLOVES tucked in your layers near your skin!

BODY HEAT will DRY 'em!

Now what do I do to dry out? First, when I get into camp I put on a bunch of layers while I am still warm. This is a good idea whenever you stop because it's better to trap the heat you have then to let it escape. If you let yourself get cold before layering up, you have to regenerate the warmth you lost. You worked hard to create all that body heat; don't waste it. By staying warm, your body starts to act like a clothes dryer. Your warmth pushes the moisture away from your body into successively outer layers of clothing and eventually the air. How fast this happens depends on how warm a person you are and how much heat you push. To help this process along you need to be active, as activity creates heat. As always, being well fed and hydrated helps too.

Once in camp with some layers on, I do the work that needs to get done. This usually involves some form of moving snow; digging shelters, building kitchens or making improvements. By staying busy and keeping warm I usually dry out my clothes by the time bedtime rolls around.

If smaller items, such as gloves and socks, have not dried out by the time I am ready for bed, I sleep with them in my bag to dry them out.

FROZEN BOOTS!

Since wet or damp wool socks freeze in the winter, you need to be active to dry them out. Once you take them off, put them on your shoulders next to your wicking layer. This keeps them warm and with time they will dry out. Since it takes time for wool to dry, you may need to sleep with your socks. I usually keep a pair on my shoulders and put the other pairs on my stomach or along the inside of my thighs. I can dry four socks a night. Be careful though, and don't try and dry too much stuff in your bag at night. This can rob you of heat and make your night unpleasant. Another option is to put wet socks over a hot water bottle and sleep with it. This works to dry socks although it stretches them out a bit.

The same is true for boots. As boots get wet from sweat they start to freeze when they are off your feet. This makes it a real drag to put them back on your feet. You need to find a way to keep them warm. At night it is easy enough to sleep with them

X-RAY VIEW
of
SKI BOOTS

these need to be
kept from freezing!
So tie 'em
together and wear
'em under your
PARKA!

in your bag; other times, tie the laces together and suspend them around your neck underneath your parka. A small whisk brush is invaluable for cleaning the snow out of those hard to reach places on your boots. This keeps the snow from melting in your bag. An advantage to double boots, besides being warmer, is that you can sleep with just the inner boot and leave the bulkier shells out. If you wear glasses, you may find that your boots also make a great place to put your lenses at night.

Gaiters and anything nylon (like wind shells) dry quickly in the winter. For this reason I don't go to great lengths to dry this stuff at night. If I want to keep it from freezing I stick it under or between my sleeping pads.

Finally, whenever the sun is shining you can dry wet stuff. If you are not wearing your boots, put them in the sun, with the insoles pulled out. If you have glue-on skins, hang them off your skis to dry. Put those frozen water bottles out. Use those sunny days to your advantage but be careful to not let things blow away if the wind comes up. As you become skilled at winter camping, you will find it easier and easier to keep stuff dry and to dry it out when it does get wet.

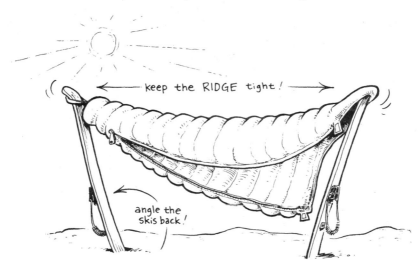

keep the RIDGE tight!

angle the
skis back!

TIP FOR SLEEPING BAGS
Sleeping bags absorb moisture from our bodies at night, especially when we are drying out damp clothes. To keep them dry, hang them on your skis in the morning as soon as you get up. The warm moisture will evaporate out of your bag in the cold dry air. This works especially well in the wind. Even if it is snowing you can do this as long as it is not a warm wet snowfall. Dry snow easily brushes off without making the bag wet.

CAMPING IN THE SNOW

SNOW SHELTERS

Perhaps nothing about winter camping is as distinctive as the ability to build with snow. The presence of this amazing stuff gives us the opportunity to build truly comfy winter shelters. A snow shelter is warmer and quieter then a tent, a big advantage on windy nights. They can be small enough for one person or big enough to accommodate 20 people. Once you have gained the know-how and have some experience under your belt, they become relatively easy to build.

There are many different types of snow shelters and each has its advantages and disadvantages. Some work only in certain given snow conditions, while others are more adaptable. The only things you really need to build a shelter are snow, a shovel and the willingness to work hard for a couple of hours.

There are two basic principles involved with snow shelters. One is work hardening of the snow and the other is shape. In work hardening the snow we are compressing it via mechanical action, thereby making it denser and strengthening the bonds between the grains of snow. This allows us to dig in the snow without having it fall down on us and gives us the ability to cut blocks out of it. The amount of work hardening that needs to be done depends on the snow.

WORK HARDENING SNOW!

HOT and SWEATY! STRIP SOME LAYERS BEFORE YOU SOAK YOURSELF!

also

a good way to warm up...

TROMP HARD WITH YOUR SKIS and BEAT MERCILESSLY with yer POLES!

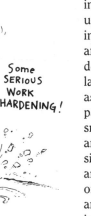

BOOT PACKING!

Some SERIOUS WORK HARDENING!

In its natural state snow settles. As this process proceeds it develops stronger bonds and becomes denser. Wind further work hardens snow by blowing it around and compacting it. This is why snow drifts tend to be so much harder than the snow around them. Often these natural processes need to be supplemented to get the snow to bond well enough to build with. This can be done by ski packing the snow or boot and/or shovel packing it. The less dense and well bonded the snow, the longer and harder you should work harden it. New snow tends to bond better than old sugar snow.

To ski pack the snow, ski around on top of it, side stepping the area you want to pack down. Ski packing only affects the top layers of the snow. Given the type of snow, i.e., denser versus lighter, we may be able to walk around on top of it without skis in a few minutes or it might take overnight to set up. Boot packing an area means walking around in the snow packing it out with our feet. This affects a deeper layer of snow and makes it denser and harder. To work harden even a deeper layer of snow, I can take my shovel and shove it as far down in the snow as I can while I boot pack. If I want to make a quarry to cut blocks for snow shelters, I first ski pack an area, then boot and shovel pack it till I can stand up without sinking in. I can also shovel in new snow from around the sides to build it up. Finally, I smooth off the surface with either my skis or my shovel and let it set up for an hour or so. Shovel packing the snow is done by shoveling snow, jabbing it with your shovel or packing the snow down with the back of your blade.

The shape of the ideal snow shelter is domed. This is the strongest shape and makes the longest-lasting shelter because snow shelters tend to sag with time. The next best thing to a dome is an arch and the smallest and largest shelters will often have straight walls and an arched ceiling. The worst snow shelters have flat ceilings or an upside down saucer shape. They sag rapidly and are more likely to collapse when being dug out.

QUINZHEES

Quinzhee is an Athapaskan word for a snow shelter that was popular in the taiga regions of the great white north. It is a shelter that can be built even when the snow pack is shallow. The shallower the snow, however, the longer it takes to pile it up for the shelter, and you may even have to transport snow to the site in a really low snow pack.

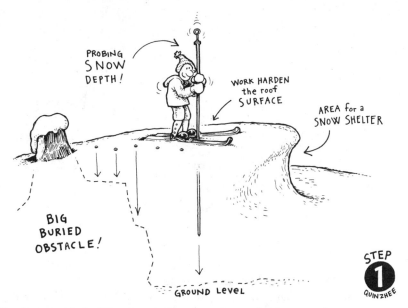

PROBING SNOW DEPTH!

WORK HARDEN the roof SURFACE

AREA for a SNOW SHELTER

BIG BURIED OBSTACLE!

GROUND LEVEL

STEP 1 QUINZHEE

The first step in building a quinzhee is to determine how much snow you have. I usually do this by probing with my skis or a probe pole. If the snow is deeper then 4 feet, a quinzhee may not be the fastest choice (see dugloos). When probing to find the deepest snow, you should also feel for what is under the snow where you eventually plan to build a winter home. Although indoor plants are nice, they do take up precious space and finding trees, logs or rocks while digging out the quinzhee is a drag. By careful probing you can assure yourself of an uncluttered site. Once this is done you can determine the size you want it to be.

STEP 2 QUINZHEE

Now the sizing of quinzhees is a personal thing, so I will just give some guidelines and you can experiment and find what works best. In general, the smaller a snow shelter is the stronger it is.

You can start with a PILE OF GEAR in the center...

PILE UP ONLY WHAT YOU WON'T NEED FOR THE NEXT COUPLE of HOURS!

this'll save a little work during "mole" time

For three people a circle with the diameter of a ski seems to work most of the time. Now you may be asking how long is this ski? I like to use the tallest person's skis. Just remember that the shorter the ski, the shorter the person, and the smaller the quinzhee can be. For every additional person, you need to add about a foot to the diameter. When you have the diameter figured out, you want to walk around the perimeter of it two or three times to boot pack the snow some. This will be the foundation for the walls. I will often stand my skis up on the outside of this circle so I can remember where it is as I pile snow.

STOMP! STOMP!

BOOT PACK and WORK HARDEN A CIRCLE

This creates a solid "FOUNDATION" for the walls.

MOUND THE SNOW
and
CREATE A DOME

DON'T DIG IN
PAST the BOOT-PACKED
"FOUNDATION"

STEP
3
QUINZHEE

Now we get to the fun part. Piling snow in the middle of the circle, piling more snow on top of this and then more snow. Then you will have to pile some more snow until you get a nice dome shape that rises from the outside of your foundation to about 4 to 6 feet in height. The shallower the snow pack the higher it should be. Once you get to this point, you need to attack it with your shovels and pack the snow down. You want it to bond well so don't be shy! Then you get to pile more snow on and repeat this process until the packed snow is at the outer limits of the shape you want. At this point you can throw on the finishing touches, get that nice domed shape and smooth it out. Then take a dinner break. That's right, go take some time and eat a good meal and get a hot drink, because part two is about to begin and you will need those calories. Plus that work-hardened snow needs about an hour or two to set up.

WHAP!
WHAP!

WORK HARDEN
the outside surface,
Be BOLD and do a
good job! This is
an important step!

STEP
4
QUINZHEE

While you are waiting, you can walk around the quinzhee and shove skis and poles into the shelter. Push them in about 18 to

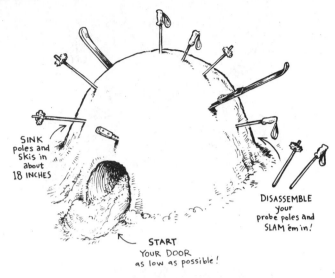

SINK
poles and
Skis in
about
18 INCHES

DISASSEMBLE
your
probe poles and
SLAM 'em'in!

START
YOUR DOOR
as low as possible!

STEP
5
QUINZHEE

24 inches. They are your markers for when you are get close to the desired wall thickness as you dig it out. Once an hour or so has gone by, you can start to excavate all that snow you threw up. First the door: Start at the perimeter of the quinzhee and dig down until you're a few inches above the ground. Then start digging the door by digging in and then up. Once again personal preference will come into play. Some like it big, some like it small. I like a big door as I hate to crawl. But you will lose more heat through a big door. One thing to remember though is that it's easy to make a door bigger but almost impossible to make it smaller again. As you start to dig the door, you will realize this is a wet proposition. To help with this, wear a minimum of layers and all your wind clothes. Keep all your spare layers handy so that when you come out you can just throw them on before you get cold. The person doing the excavation is called the "mole."

I would suggest making the door just big enough so you can dig sitting on your knees without the top of the doorway being above your head. You can always make it bigger later if you want. Once you have dug in about 16 inches you can start digging up. Now you need to be thinking about a number of important things.

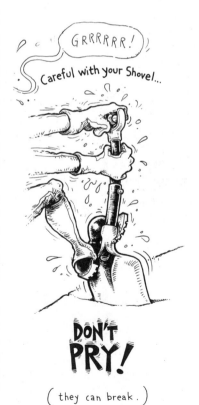

GRRRRRR!

Careful with your Shovel...

DON'T PRY!

(they can break .)

• You want the walls to be about 14 to 16 inches thick; if they get to be too thin or too thick they will sag faster. If you block the door from incoming light while you dig, you will notice that light comes through the walls at 16 inches or so. This should be a warning not to excavate more snow from these areas.

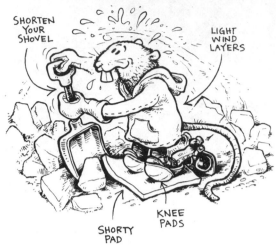

SHORTEN
YOUR
SHOVEL

LIGHT
WIND
LAYERS

KNEE
PADS

SHORTY
PAD

THE WELL DRESSED MOLE!

this is hot and active work
in a very humid setting; be
careful not to get too hot
or get chilled when done!

the spooky sound
of
SETTLING SNOW!

- You need to dig up so that you don't find yourself with a whole lot of snow over your head (i.e., more than 2 feet) because if the shelter were to collapse for some reason you don't want to be buried. For this reason it is also a good idea to always have someone at the door once you start digging inside the shelter. Not only does this person shovel out the snow you toss out the door, but they are there to dig you out should the shelter fall down. Some moles like to wear their transceivers just in case.

- The snow forming the shelter may collapse or "whumpf" as you are digging, without knocking the shelter down. In this case it is a good idea to come out and let it set up a little longer.

DON'T
DIG OUT the
sides and
leave the
weight in
the roof...
IT
COULD
SQUISH
YOU!

DON'T
let the door
fill in!

DEPTH meters

KEEP the door clear of snow!

IT IS EASIEST to stand and Dig...

FILL IN THE STANDING AREA at the end with the final Volume of snow!

STEP 6 QUINZHEE

• Dig standing up as much as possible to stay drier. As you go, dig out the snow from the ceiling to the ground. You achieve maximum head room this way. You can build the sleeping platform at the end with the last of the snow you take off the walls.

• Try to make the walls as smooth as possible, and above all else keep it dome shaped.

When the snow pack is deeper then 2 feet I build the shelter with a sleeping platform. If the platform is higher then the top of the door, it creates a heat trap and the shelter will be warm. I have never been to fond of these because they just fog my glasses up. Any raised platform creates a cold sink out the door and makes the shelter warmer so I tend not to worry about it being above the door. This way I don't need to crawl through the door either. But remember it is just personal choice and

poke some VENT HOLES

MAKE YOUR KITCHEN in the area you've already dug out!

Keep a SHOVEL INSIDE

HEAT TRAP the floor is above the door

COMPLETED 7 QUINZHEE

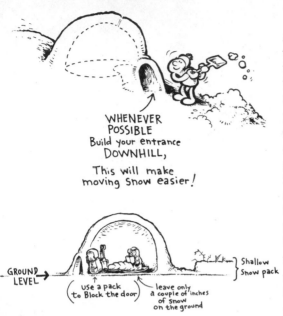

WHENEVER
POSSIBLE
Build your entrance
DOWNHILL,

This will make
moving Snow easier!

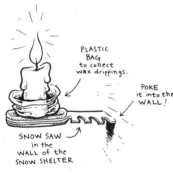

GROUND
LEVEL →

use a pack
to Block the door

leave only
a couple of inches
of snow
on the ground

Shallow
Snow pack

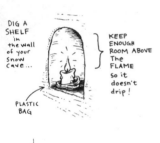

DIG A
SHELF
in
the wall
of your
snow
cave...

KEEP
ENOUGH
ROOM ABOVE
The
FLAME
So it
doesn't
drip!

PLASTIC
BAG

PLASTIC
BAG
to collect
wax drippings.

POKE
it into the
WALL!

SNOW SAW
in the
WALL of the
SNOW SHELTER

some folks really like the heat trap. Also with a deeper snow pack you can build the shelter on a hillside. Put the door on the downhill side. This facilitates snow removal.

If the snow pack is shallow, do away with the platform and sleep closer to the earth; this means less shoveling and will give you more room. The temperature at the ground during the winter stays around 32 degrees and is warmer than the outside air temperature. Leave a couple of inches of snow on the floor to protect the plants near the ground.

Vents are poked with ski poles in the walls of the quinzhee to keep it from becoming steamy and wet.

If it gets dark out while you are building, a candle works great to light up the inside of a quinzhee. Also once you smooth out your floor give it a little time to set up. The warmth from the candle will help with this as well. While the quinzhee is going up, the stove can be melting water for dinner, hot drinks and so on. The person moling the quinzhee out is likely to get quite wet and therefore it is a good idea to pump them with hot water and food. Once a shelter is done, it is very rare for them to collapse. They just tend to get stronger. In fact, you can normally walk on top of them after a couple of days. What usually destroys a snow shelter is time. The snow will eventually sag down until there is no more shelter. With time and practice you will get faster at digging these shelters. I have built a quinzhee in less than two hours but I have also seen it take up to six. Plan on going slow until you gain more experience with them. Some people fly or tent camp the first night and build the shelter the next day.

DUGLOOS AND IGLOOS

Both of these shelters require the use of blocks, which means that in addition to a shovel you will need a snow saw. If the snow is hard enough to stand on, you can just cut blocks directly from it. If not, you need to make a quarry. For a dugloo you should work harden an area a ski length by a pole length. For an igloo, make it a ski by two skis. This gives you some room for error. Let your quarry set up for at least an hour and don't step on it or you may put cracks into it. Next, you need to dig a trench around two sides of your quarry and smooth off these sides. The longest side will be the front. Now you are ready to begin cutting blocks.

THE FINE ART OF BLOCK CUTTING

Make blocks that are the handle of the saw wide, the full saw in length and a saw blade in depth. First cut the back, then cut this into lengths and lastly cut along the bottom. When cutting out the blocks make sure to use smooth even strokes. Rushing through the process makes incomplete cuts. You should notice the block drop down while finishing the last cut. If not run the saw through the cuts again. By placing the saw behind the blocks you can carefully tilt them forward until you can pick them up. Be careful picking up and moving blocks as they are fragile. The more time they sit after having been cut the stronger they become.

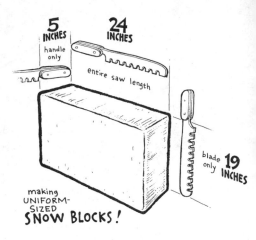

making UNIFORM-SIZED **SNOW BLOCKS!**

work hardened
QUARRY for SNOW BLOCKS

IGLOOS

These are fun but are not the most efficient structures to build unless you have hard snow. They are the most challenging of all the structures to build, so be patient. There are also many ways to go about building them, but I will limit myself to the one with which I am familiar. Start out on a ski-packed surface by making a circle the radius of a ski pole, about 130 centimeters in length. This should fit about three people. A great way to get a nice circle is to mark the middle of your igloo site by planting a pole there. Now slip the strap of the other pole over it and scribe out a circle with it. It is important to have a good circular shape.

Now you can start laying the blocks out. Any block can be supported by two diagonally opposite corners. This is the basis of block setting. A third corner helps hold the block in position. Getting the corners to stick to the previous blocks is the biggest challenge. This is called sintering the

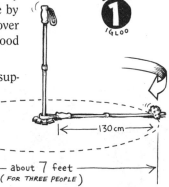

STEP **1** IGLOO

130 cm

about 7 feet
(FOR THREE PEOPLE)

CHECK IT OUT!
these snow blocks can be nicely balanced by just two points...
and
this is important when building a round structure with RECTANGULAR blocks!

thre SINTER POINTS OF

HOW TO MAKE YOUR FIRST BLOCKS

MAKE SURE THE BLOCKS TILT INWARD!

corners because that's the name of the process in which snow crystals bond together.

To start, cut a block into two unequal halves and lay the halves along the outside of your circle. Help sinter the corners by tapping the block slightly and blowing on the corners. It is important to hold the blocks in place until they are self-supporting. Keep laying blocks around the circle until the first row or course is complete. These blocks should all lean toward the middle of the circle. The next course will spiral up the ramp you created with the first block. Be patient with these blocks and give them plenty of time to sinter. You should expect to drop some or have one fall out of place when you thought it was set. It is important that each new course have more lean toward the center than the previous row!

As you set these blocks you will notice that they leave bigger and bigger triangular spaces behind. This is perfectly okay. When the last block has been laid on top you can come back and "chink" all these holes with leftover and broken blocks. During the first row of blocks you should cut an extra long one that will span the space where the door goes. Keep spiraling up and checking that each block tilts or leans in more then the one in row below it. This is where the domed shape comes from. If you don't get enough lean, you will either wind up with a turret or a volcano, neither of which you want.

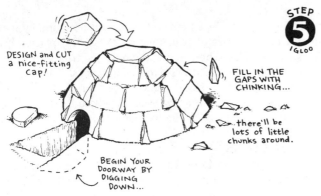

DESIGN and CUT a nice-fitting cap!

FILL IN THE GAPS WITH CHINKING...

...there'll be lots of little chunks around.

BEGIN YOUR DOORWAY BY DIGGING DOWN...

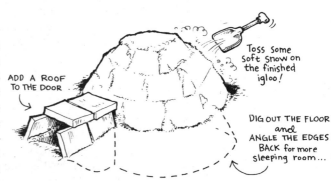

As you are laying the blocks you want to shovel the floor down one to two feet, bevel the walls out for more room and put in the door. At some point, you need to stockpile some blocks inside the igloo, as this is easier than passing them in through the door. By about your fourth row you should be getting ready to close

ADD A ROOF TO THE DOOR

Toss some soft snow on the finished igloo!

DIG OUT THE FLOOR and ANGLE THE EDGES BACK for more sleeping room...

COMPLETED
6
IGLOO!

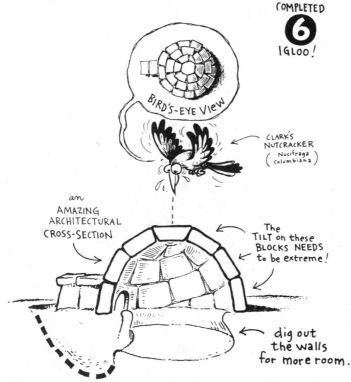

BIRD'S-EYE VIEW

CLARK'S NUTCRACKER
(Nucifraga columbiana)

an AMAZING ARCHITECTURAL CROSS-SECTION

The TILT on these BLOCKS NEEDS to be extreme!

dig out the walls for more room.

it off. One or two blocks cut to fit and laid horizontally make up this cap. Be careful maneuvering these into place. Often times you can place the block in the hole and trim it fit by sawing along the joint with the surrounding blocks. It should drop into to place with a slight thud. Once you finish chinking, throw a dusting of light snow over the whole thing. It should take between 20 to 24 blocks to complete an igloo this size.

DUGLOOS

This snow shelter is a dome-shaped cavity in the snow, dug by starting at the top and then capped with blocks. It is faster to build than a quinzhee when there is a deep snow pack because there is no piling of snow, and you only need to cut a few blocks. First probe to see how deep the snow is; it should be more than 4 feet. Also make sure there are no buried objects. Next ski pack the snow where you want to build. One person then starts to dig down in the middle of the ski packed area. This is the middle of the dugloo. Meanwhile someone else can be building the quarry, starting the stove and so on. The person digging in the middle wants a hole just big enough to get the shovel out easily. Keeping it small (less than 3 feet in diameter) will make "capping" the structure easier. Once the person digging gets down 2 feet or so, he or she can start to "bell" the structure out. Once again, shoot for that dome shape.

At this point figure out a place for the door. If you are on an incline then it should be on the downhill side. Locating the

FIND A SPOT DOWNHILL FOR THE DOOR

The CAP in the DOME is nice 'cuz YOU CAN STAND UP!

COMPLETED

3

DUGLOO

door just over a pole length away from the edge of the hole should work, it is better to begin too far away than too close because it is a lot easier to move the entranceway closer. A second person can begin work on this.

KEEP YOUR HOLE SMALL enough so it's EASY TO CAP

LEAVE A SUPPORTIVE COLUMN UNTIL THE END, You'll need to pass the Blocks to the middleman.

←DOOR

Keep a little platform to stand on or you'll be too low to throw the snow out.

The person doming should leave at least a foot of snow between the top of the dome and the top of the snow to support the blocks when they are laid. After it is capped this can be thinned down to a few inches. Also leave a 2-foot-wide pillar or undomed section of the shelter. Blocks can be passed along here instead of through the door.

To cap the dugloo you need three to four blocks and some chinking material. If you kept the hole small then you can lean two blocks together in a wide A frame and chink the ends. If not, you still shouldn't need the elaborate spiral of an igloo. By setting the blocks with lots of lean to begin with, you should be able to cap it by the fourth one. Then chink away and cover the whole affair with a light layer of snow. To finish, shovel out the pillar, shave the walls down to a nice smooth dome and work harden the floor.

CAPPING YOUR DUGLOO!

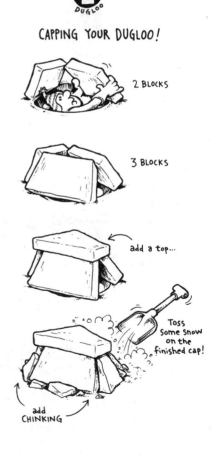

2 BLOCKS

3 BLOCKS

add a top...

Toss some snow on the finished cap!

add CHINKING

DOG HOUSES

Dog houses are quick, easy, one-person shelters. To build one you simply dig a trench deep enough to sit up in, with a tunnel for your legs so you can lay down in it. You can cap the top of the trench with an A frame of blocks, or lay skis and poles across the top and cover with a tarp or space blanket followed by snow.

SNOW CAVES

A snow cave is similar in design to a quinzhee, but you don't need to pile any snow because there is already 6 feet of snow on the ground. Look for big snow drifts or probe around to find the deepest snow pack. I avoid drifts formed by ridges or gullies as they tend to drift in very fast when it is windy and it takes a lot of shoveling to keep the door clear.

If the snow is soft, ski pack the top of the area you wish to dig, otherwise just start digging. It is a good idea to probe from the inside every once in awhile to see how close to the surface you are. Ideally you would like your ceiling to be about 2 feet thick. Once again you are shooting for that all important dome shape, but if you want to build a really big one, then dig it as a long arching hallway. With a really deep snow pack and a lot of ambition, you can make some very elaborate snow caves with separate rooms, benches for sleeping on and so forth. It is important to punch vent holes into the ceilings of snow caves to ensure enough air flow. Ski poles work well for this.

I am not much for stoves and lanterns in caves. Candles work just as well as a lantern and present no danger of a Kevorkian style death. As for stoves I prefer to cook outside or build an alcove or igloo with minimal chinking. If you do choose to cook in your shelter, it is very important do it in a well-ventilated area and build a dome, as a hood, directly above the stove with a chimney.

PROBE that SNOW DRIFT before digging your SNOW CAVE

there could be some BIG ROCKS in there!

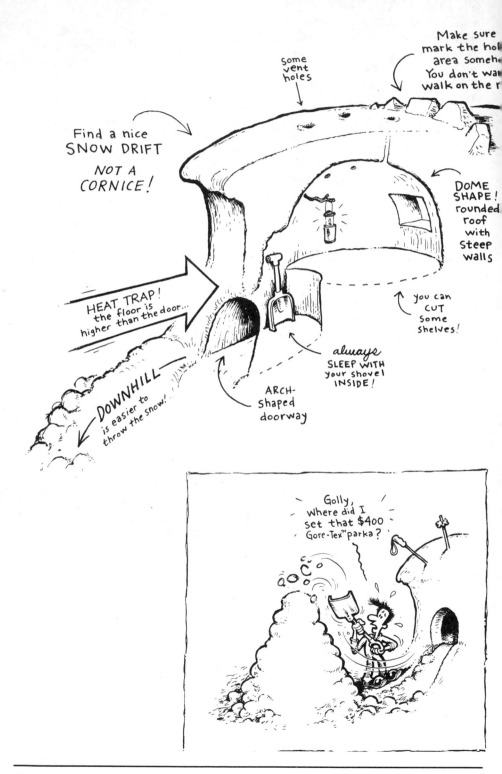

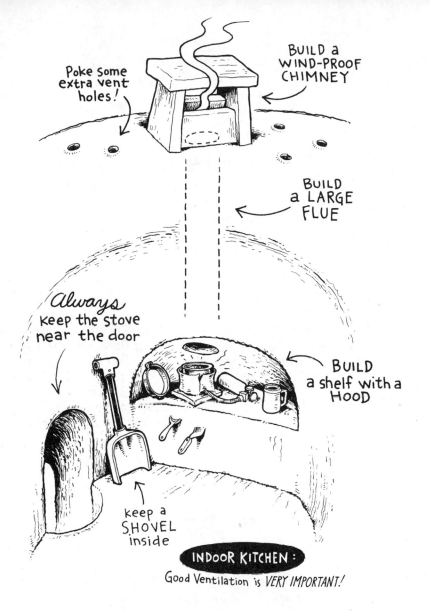

Poke some extra vent holes!

BUILD a WIND-PROOF CHIMNEY

BUILD a LARGE FLUE

Always keep the stove near the door

BUILD a shelf with a HOOD

keep a SHOVEL inside

INDOOR KITCHEN:

Good Ventilation is *VERY IMPORTANT!*

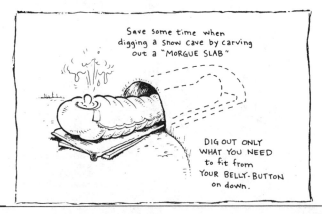

Save some time when digging a snow cave by carving out a "MORGUE SLAB"

DIG OUT ONLY WHAT YOU NEED to fit from YOUR BELLY-BUTTON on down.

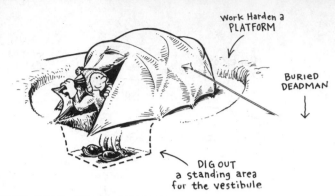

Work Harden a **PLATFORM**

BURIED DEADMAN ↓

DIG OUT a standing area for the vestibule

TENTS AND FLYS

Although not true snow shelters, tents and flys definitely have their place in winter camping. They are fast to set up and are great for single night camps or for people who don't want to go through all the work of building a snow shelter. Tents are especially easy. All you need to do is ski pack a platform, set up the tent and stake it down well.

Staking things out in the snow is a little different than staking out in the ground. For one, regular stakes won't work in most snow conditions and when placed in the conventional way, they tend to melt out, leaving your shelter vulnerable to the wind. You do have some alternatives though. You can use your skis and poles as stakes if you are just making camp for the night and know you won't be needing them, or use deadmen.

You can deadman anything that you won't have any use for— stuff sacks, extra fuel bottles, etc. While digging my kitchen, if I can find sticks or branches that have blown off trees , I prefer to use them since I won't have to dig them back up. Don't break them off the poor trees, however. The advantage of deadmen is that they won't melt out if buried deep enough.

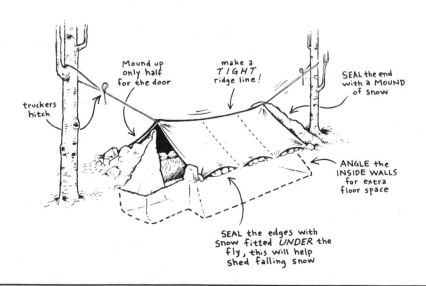

truckers hitch

Mound up only half for the door

make a *TIGHT* ridge line!

SEAL the end with a MOUND of snow

ANGLE the INSIDE WALLS for extra floor space

SEAL the edges with snow fitted *UNDER* the fly, this will help shed falling snow

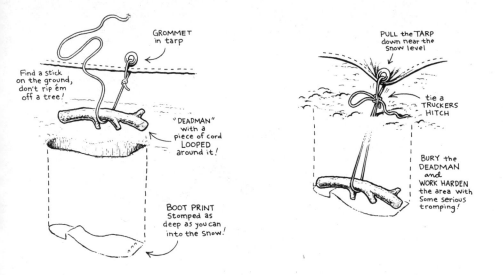

GROMMET in tarp

Find a stick on the ground, don't rip 'em off a tree!

"DEADMAN" with a piece of cord LOOPED around it!

BOOT PRINT Stomped as deep as you can into the snow!

PULL the TARP down near the snow level

tie a TRUCKERS HITCH

BURY the DEADMAN and WORK HARDEN the area with some serious tromping!

Flys work well in the winter and are lighter than tents, although they are not quite as easy to set up. With the traditional fly design, I like to ski pack out an area between two trees, set up the fly and then dig a beveled trench underneath to increase the amount of room. With the snow I dig up, I close off the two ends and the sides until it is completely sealed except for a door. It is a good idea to pitch the sides of the fly at a steep angle so snow will slide off. Failure to do this during a snow storm can result in the occupants "sucking nylon" during the night as the fly collapses on them.

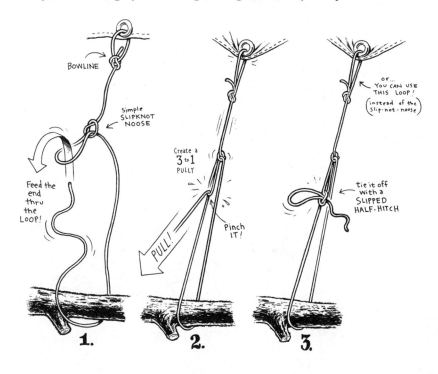

BOWLINE

Simple SLIPKNOT NOOSE

Feed the end thru the LOOP!

Create a 3 to 1 PULLY

PULL!

Pinch IT!

1.

2.

or... YOU CAN USE THIS LOOP! (instead of the slip-not-noose)

tie it off with a SLIPPED HALF-HITCH

3.

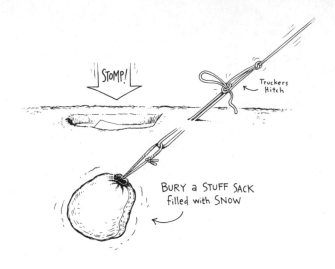

STOMP!

Truckers Hitch

BURY a STUFF SACK filled with SNOW

If you are using a megamid, try pitching it with a string between two trees. This will do away with the pole (which will sink into the snow anyway unless you have some type of platform for it). You can also seal off the sides of this and dig down to increase roominess.

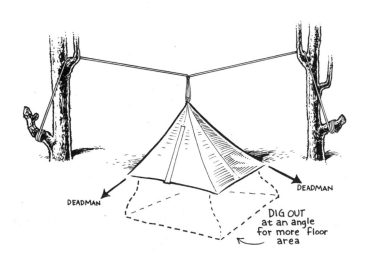

DEADMAN

DEADMAN

DIG OUT at an angle for more floor area

MINIMUM IMPACT AND OTHER BACKCOUNTRY ETHICS

A simple equation exists between freedom and numbers: the more people the less freedom.

Basic Rockcraft by Royal Robbins

Ethics can be seen as set of principles or standards that help govern the actions of a community. In our case, these ethics can help define proper behavior for skiers in the backcountry. This covers a lot of ground and not all these standards are accepted everywhere. But by having high ethical standards we can stave off regulation meant to modify irresponsible behavior. With increased use of the backcountry, we are beginning to see government agencies and private citizens consider regulations to protect it and its users. Wouldn't it be better to govern ourselves through the use of ethics? This allows for flexibility rather than having to follow a set of unbending rules.

Some of what I discuss here is just plain courtesy to others, while other issues are of a more serious nature. All in all, it's worth the time to consider and to accept those things that ring true to you. If you are unsure of something then give it a try, ask opinions of others and do some research. Don't just blow it off as the opinion of some mad man. By education, we learn more about the true nature of things. In addition to being of an ethical nature, much of the following are just good backcountry skills to understand and practice.

Minimum impact skills are meant to protect backcountry areas that are seeing more and more use and to give each person the chance to experience the backcountry on his or her own terms. By practicing minimum impact, we decrease our impact on the land and all the associated things that go with it such as water, animals, plants, etc. We also strive to lessen the impact we have on other users in the backcountry. In turn, it is hoped they will do the same for us.

Once upon a time, three friends and myself were getting ready to descend a north-facing bowl on skis after having done a great climb up the northeast ridge. We had been having a great climb up the northeast ridge. We had been having a great day and were looking forward to our planned descent. While digging a snow pit to assess the avalanche potential of the slope, three snowmobilers arrived in the area. They decided to high point in the exact bowl we were hoping to ski, despite the fact there were numerous similar options in the same vicinity. It would be an understatement to say we didn't appreciate their zooming around us as we put on our skis. To add insult to injury they all sat at the bottom of the bowl as we skied down, hootin' and hollerin' whenever someone fell, which wasn't hard given the difficult snow conditions created by their tracks. A day that had started off so nice, which we had hoped to cap off with this 900-foot vertical descent, had been ruined. It is thoughtless acts like these that have turned me off to snowmobilers.

As backcountry skiers we need to think about how our actions will be interpreted by others. Otherwise we may find that others will view us in a negative light.

SANITATION AND WASTE

Yikes! This is a scary section to write as "waste" is not an everyday topic of discussion for most of us. Yet it is a an everyday part of our lives, and we need to know how to deal with this messy stuff when we are out there in the backcountry, away from all our modern conveniences. Developing the skills to deal successfully with minimizing our impact on the land and others starts here.

"PACK IT IN, PACK IT OUT"

There it is again, that old familiar maxim. Just because there are no trash cans around doesn't mean we can toss our garbage in the snow and ski off. Litter is litter and there is no excuse for leaving it behind in the winter or at any other time. "Out of sight out of mind" is no longer acceptable in today's busy wilderness areas. No matter where you are somebody is sure to stumble onto your trash, so develop a system for taking care of it. I like to keep a small plastic bag handy for those little scraps of garbage that invariably appear throughout the day. Keep a garbage bag in the food bag for all the garbage and waste that is associated with cooking meals. This system pretty much covers it all and makes collection of litter easy. If you were strong enough to carry it in then taking it back out shouldn't be any problem.

Shovel as BALANCE POINT
(Don't fall!)

DON'T POOP on your BOOTS!

← AIM!

"TOILET PAPER" handy.

Work harden a nice Stable platform!

HUMAN WASTE

Now here is a real sensitive issue. What do we do with our poop? Contamination of water sources by human fecal matter is a serious and growing concern. Waterborne illnesses such as giardiasis and campylobacter are present in many of the streams and lakes in the backcountry. Although we may not be the original reason for these microorganisms existence in these waters, we are a major carrier of pathogens, and there is no reason for us to contribute more to this. For this reason it is important we dispose of our waste properly. Plus we don't want to bum out other users in the spring with our foul dirt.

So what do we do in the winter? Well, with 4 feet of snow it's not practical to dig to the ground, and even if we did it would be hard to dig up the frozen earth to dispose of our dump. The best answer, next to packing it out, is to leave it up near the snow's surface where the action of freezing and thawing during the cycle of day and night will break it down and kill the pathogens in it. In addition, the snow dilutes it as it melts in the spring. For the freeze-thaw action to work best we need to choose areas that have a southerly exposure for maximum sunshine. Also keep in mind, there is always a chance that other people will come into an area before your dump has disappeared. For this reason try and locate a place that is off the paths of travel.

Maybe now is a good time for a rendition of how to poop in the woods in the winter. First off, it's a good idea to figure out what your schedule is. There is nothing worse than being caught with your boots off, especially since you need to ski out of camp to find a good location to properly disperse your dump. With some prethought you may have already packed out a trail to a nice area that you can boot to, but most likely skiing is your best option. I like to ski a couple of minutes out of camp. This ensures I am not concentrating a bunch of dumps in one area.

DON'T POOP on yer Skis!   TOILET PAPER, all ready

the
WALK
into the
WOODS:

1. BE READY!
2. PLAN AHEAD.
3. GET OUT OF VIEW of other campers.
4. PICK A GOOD SPOT!

TIC! TIC! TIC!

a nice FIRM BLOCK of "TOILET PAPER"

(remember:)
YOU'LL MOVE SLOWLY walking in deep snow!

Now look for a spot that is south facing, away from any potential drainage's by at least 200 feet and that has a nice view. (One should never underestimate a "room with a view.") I like to stomp out a nice flat platform with my skis and take my pole and make a hole in the snow. This is my target. After finishing my duty I cover up the hole so as to reduce its visual impact. As spring comes along the snow melts down and a freeze-thaw regime begins.

Natural toilet paper is abundant in the winter. Snow makes an exceptional wiping material. If you can make a good snowball out of it, you are all set. With dry powder snow it is best to use snow that has been work hardened. I often cut some blocks with my saw from the snow kitchen and take them with me on my morning "walk." If the idea of snow absolutely appalls you, using real TP is fine as long as you pack it out! It is impossible to completely burn TP in the snow and leaving it behind is worse than litter. Simply having a plastic bag to put the used product in works great. This can be tossed when you reach civilization.

When it comes to urinating in the winter, it's pretty much acceptable anywhere. I like to pee in a few designated spots around camp though to avoid possible contamination of snow for making water. It also looks nicer when you concentrate the urine in one spot instead of having yellow pee stains everywhere you look. It's also a nice

the BARE-HANDED METHOD:
1. grab a handfull of soft snow,

2. SQUEEZE!

VOILÀ!
3. "Toilet paper" with a nice wiping point...

NOTICE: This technique ain't gunna work too well with cold, dry, noncohesive snow!
good luck!

MAKING "TOILET PAPER"

1) CHOP IT UP... *before you need it!*
2) make nice pointy shapes...
3) don't get shit on the shovel!

practice to kick a little clean white snow over pee spots; visual aesthetics count for a lot.

SANITATION

Although not really an ethical dilemma, poor sanitary practices can lead to the mung (diarrhea and its associated symptoms). This will destroy any happy campers trip into the hinterlands. Yet simple awareness and good sanitary habits can save you from grief.

For hygiene purposes, I like to use separate pairs of gloves for cooking and for pooping. This helps ensure that I won't contaminant dinner and make all my friends sick. You can also wash your hands in the snow with vigorous rubbing but this is a cold task. Some folks I know like to bathe as well in the winter. I can't say that I have ever been tempted to take a snow bath, but apparently if you choose a warm sunny day it's not a painful experience.

Keep pots, pans and dishes clean. Although this is not as important in the winter as in the summer, it lessens the chances for foodborne illnesses to develop and get passed around. Since the winter environment provides ample refrigeration, you can save leftovers. I like to fry these up for the next meal as an appetizer.

keep Hat and Sunblock ready

insulate them knees

Washin' yer face with snow

Just try and burn that toilet paper in winter!

PRESERVING THE SNOW
AND THE TRACKS

Although not an issue that affects the land, powder conservation is more and more important in backcountry areas that see a lot of use. Where I ski in the Tetons everyone wants to ski untracked powder. While it may not always be possible to get first tracks in a bowl it is usually possible to ski an untracked line if the people before you showed some consideration. By this we mean when you ski a line, try and keep it as tight as possible. One person making turns and traverses all the way across a bowl can totally ruin it for those who follow, whereas a large number of people can claim untracked lines by "spooning" close to other tracks.

In the same vein, when you are putting in an uptrack, don't put it in the middle of a bowl. Try and locate it in the trees or in an area that is not prime for skiing down. Also, because we spend more time on the uptrack than in skiing down, it needs to be in the safest terrain from possible avalanches. To be considerate I also like to put in tracks that are easy for others to

follow. Steep enough to be efficient but not so steep that it is impossible for most folks to climb. Especially since the more skiers who go up it the harder packed it gets, and this makes it even harder for skins to stick. This also helps ensure that only one up track gets broken.

For aesthetic reasons, crossing someone else's track is frowned on. One of the beauties of skiing in the backcountry is the ability to look back at your track. Many people consider the line of turns to be something of an art form. The ability to ski a good line is then seen as artistic expression. For others to unthinkingly ski over these tracks is bad form. Think about painting a slope.

WILDLIFE

Large animals have it rough in the winter. It's cold out there and most of their food sources are buried under the snow. To survive they must conserve their resources. We don't help them out if we continually disturb them. If you do happen to come across moose or elk, don't make them exhaust their energy by continually running away. Give them plenty of space and try to avoid disturbing them more. Take pleasure in that initial encounter but don't press on trying to get a better look.

DOGS

I can understand why people like to take their dogs with them. It's a chance to give the dog some exercise and to explore that special companionship that exists between humans and canines. Although I have no trouble with this, there are problems that I have seen with dogs and skiing. Yappy dogs can be annoying to others trying to enjoy the peacefulness of winter. In spite of what many dog owners think, not everyone loves dogs. I myself used to be a dog owner, but the preponderance of dogs where I ski has diminished my fondness for the beasts—the owners not the dogs. One problem is the amount of dog poop that accumulates on the major travel corridors. It's like a minefield out there, folks. Dog owners should take responsibility to clean up after their pets. Shoveling the poop into a dense group of trees would be a good start.

Another thing that concerns me are those owners who have no idea where their dog is. Time and time again I have met people who have no idea where their dog is and dogs who have no idea where their owner is. If you are more concerned with your skiing than with keeping track of your dog, leaving the dog at home might be a better answer to burdening others with the task of keeping an eye out for it.

Now if all the dogs out there were trained avalanche dogs I would be psyched. Unfortunately they're not, but fortunately not all dogs or their owners cause problems.

PREPAREDNESS

An ethical standard that seems to be missing from a lot of peoples consciousness is that of self-responsibility. If we choose to venture into the backcountry, we need to realize that in making this decision we are assuming the risks and responsibilities associated with that choice. We cannot expect others to come to our rescue. We certainly cannot not blame anyone else for our actions or inactions. It is our responsibility to be prepared. It is also our responsibility to use our heads. That's what that gray matter is for.

When you go skiing bring your shovel, transceiver, pack with extra layers and so on. Learn how to use all that stuff. Make sure your buddies are equally prepared. What if they have to dig you out? A transceiver is nothing but an annoying box that beeps if you don't know how to use it. Even when I ski solo I bring all this stuff. Then I know I can be of help to others should I come across a bad situation. I hope others would do the same for me.

Be conservative. There is an old saying "live to wimp again." There is no reason to end your ski season early. If you die then that's the last run you ever get.

Educate yourself. It's hard to avoid avalanche terrain if you don't know what it looks like. The same goes for cold injuries and so on. You may never know it all, but by continuing the learning process you continue to grow and expand your potential.

Finally don't be afraid to take risks. Risk taking is what makes life fun and interesting. But take appropriate risks so life stays fun and interesting. Take responsibility for your actions. Skiing in the backcountry is a wonderful sport and hopefully something we can do for a long long time.

OTHER CHALLENGES

Once you have mastered the basics of winter camping and skiing, what can you do for your next challenge? There are a number of things: long winter expeditions, mountain ski descents, extreme skiing and ice cap traverses. Anything is within reach if you want to put forth the effort. There are hut routes to do in Colorado. High mountain traverses in the Sierras. Ski descents of the Northwest's volcanoes and much more.

If you plan to ski on glaciers, then you should be aware that while skis spread out your weight and make crevasse falls less likely, they only make them less likely. Having the skills to travel safely in crevassed terrain is very important. Skiing roped on glaciers is "expert stuff," especially descents, which is why some people decide to take the risk of skiing unroped when descending. In this case it is good to be able to recognize where the most heavily crevassed terrain is so that you can avoid it. Come to think of it, I always try to avoid going where the majority of crevasses are.

I can't claim to be an extreme skier, but I do know that for ski descents on steep terrain being able to self-arrest is a handy skill. Long slides on corn snow or any other snow are best avoided. Not only do you lose precious turns, but if you are out of control the possibility of getting hurt increases. Injuries diminish your ski time and are best avoided.

As for ice caps I'll let you in on the secret that there are more than just those at the poles. Take a look at a map and start planning. There is a whole world of wonderful skiing out there, from day trips, to skiing the untracked regions beyond the crowds, to doing expeditions somewhere in the remote areas of the globe. Go get it!

APPENDIX A

TOURING SETUP
- ❑ Wicking layer top and bottom
- ❑ Upper body layers (insulating) (2 to 4)
- ❑ Lower body layer (insulating) (1)
- ❑ Wind shirt and pants
- ❑ Warm hat
- ❑ Neck gaiter
- ❑ Gloves and or mittens (shelled)
- ❑ Sunglasses and sunscreen
- ❑ Socks
- ❑ Boots
- ❑ Gaiters
- ❑ Skis
- ❑ Poles
- ❑ Skins
- ❑ Transceiver
- ❑ Shovel
- ❑ Day pack
- ❑ Shortie pad
- ❑ Water bottle or Thermos
- ❑ Food
- ❑ First aid/emergency gear
- ❑ Wax kit
- ❑ Maps

❑ MISCELLANEOUS ITEMS
- ❑ Heel lifts
- ❑ Knee pads
- ❑ Probe
- ❑ Slope meter

CAMPING SETUP
- ❑ *THIS BOOK*!
- ❑ Heavy parka
- ❑ Insulated pants
- ❑ Extra socks (2 to 3)
- ❑ Extra gloves and mitts (1 to 2 each)
- ❑ Bootie system
- ❑ Overboots or mukluks
- ❑ Brush for snow
- ❑ Sleeping bag
- ❑ Ensolite pads/Thermarest (2)
- ❑ Stove and stove pad
- ❑ Lighters or matches
- ❑ Pot and pot pad
- ❑ Fry pan
- ❑ Utensils
- ❑ Cup/bowl/spoon
- ❑ Food bag
- ❑ Fuel
- ❑ Snow saw
- ❑ Headlamp
- ❑ Candles
- ❑ Pack and or sled
- ❑ Tarp or tent
- ❑ Beefed up repair and first aid kit
- ❑ Toothbrush, etc.
- ❑ Zip bag for organization

MISCELLANEOUS ITEMS
- ❑ Lantern
- ❑ Extra hat
- ❑ Bivy sack
- ❑ Water purification
- ❑ Pee bottle

APPENDIX B

OTHER WINTER RESOURCES

Daffern, Tony. *Avalanche Safety for Skiers and Climbers.* Cloudcap, Seattle, WA, 1992. 192 pages

Dunn, John M. *Winterwise: A Backpackers Guide.* The Adirondack Mountain Club, Lake George, NY, 1988. 182 pages.

Fredston, Jill, and Doug Fesler. *Snow Sense.* Alaska Mountain Safety Center, Inc., Anchorage, AK, 1994. 116 pages

Halfpenny, James C., and Roy Douglas Ozanne. *Winter an Ecological Handbook.* Johnson Books, Boulder, CO. 1989. 273 pages.

Hampton, Bruce, and David Cole. *Soft Paths.* Stackpole Books, Mechanicsburg, PA, 1995. 222 pages.

McClung, David., Schaerer, Peter. *The Avalanche Handbook.* The Mountaineers, Seattle, WA, 1993. 271 pages.

Moynier, John. *Avalanche Awareness.* Chockstone Press, Evergreen, CO, 1993. 32 pages.

Parker, Paul. *Freehill Skiing.* Chelsea Green Publishing Company, Chelsea, VT, 1988. 172 pages.

Powers, Phil. *NOLS Wilderness Mountaineering.* Stackpole Books, Mechanicsburg, PA, 1993. 241 pages.

Schimelpfenig, Tod, and Linda Lindsey. *NOLS Wilderness First Aid.* Stackpole Books, Harrisburg, PA, 1992. 356 pages.

Selters, Andy. *Glacier Travel and Crevasse Rescue.* The Mountaineers, Seattle, WA,1990. 159 pages.

Tejada-Flores, Lito. *Backcountry Skiing.* Sierra Club Books, San Francisco, CA, 1981. 306 pages.

The NOLS Cookery. Sukey Richard, Donna Orr and Claudia Lindholm, eds. The National Outdoor Leadership School and Stackpole Books, Harrisburg, PA, 1991. 106 pages.

Wilkerson, James A. *Medicine for Mountaineering.* The Mountaineers, Seattle, WA, 1990. 438 pages.

EPIC WINTER TALES

Lansing, Alfred. *Endurance*. Carroll and Graf Publishers, New York, 1993. 282 pages.

Rawicz, Slavomir. *The Long Walk*. Lyons and Buford, Publishers, New York, 1984. 240 pages.

Service, Robert. *The Best of Robert Service*. Perigee Books, New York, 1953. 216 pages.

Huntford, Roland. *The Last Place on Earth* (originally published under the title *Scott and Amundsen*). Atheneum, New York, 1986. 565 Pages.

OUTDOOR AND WINTER SKILLS EDUCATION

National Outdoor Leadership School (NOLS)
288 Main Street, Lander, WY 82520-3128
(307) 332-6973
Web site: http://www.nols.edu

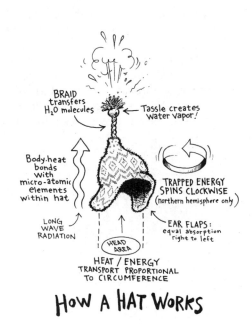

HOW A HAT WORKS

AUTHORS

Allen O'Bannon grew up in Portland, Oregon and first learned to ski on the slopes of Mount Hood. In the mid-80s he made not only a transition to the mountains of the west but also to a pair of freeheel bindings. Allen has worked for the National Outdoor Leadership School since 1987 and is a senior instructor in the NOLS winter program. Unable to find a real job, he turned to writing this book to support his ski habit. He currently resides for part of the year in Victor, Idaho and is planning a presidential campaign for 2004.

Mike Clelland never went to Art School, studying Mad Magazine instead. Mike grew up in the flat plains of Michigan, then spent ten years (as a Yuppie!) in New York City. In 1987 he thought it might be fun to be a ski bum in Wyoming for the winter. Unfortunately, after living and skiing in the Rockies, he found it quite impossible to return to his previous life in the Big City. Mike is presently living in a shed in Idaho where he divides his time between illustrator and NOLS instructor.